ADVANCE PRAISE

"Phyllis T. Morgan, visionary, academic influencer, and former OUSD Principal has a wealth of information to share in this book about how parents can set up students for success! She led the way for one of the lowest-performing schools in Oceanside to become a Distinguished School. Trust her wisdom and commit to the strategies."

– Margaret Malek, Teacher of the Year

"School is a place where information is dumped onto our students. To really learn and understand what a child needs, practical hands-on experiences can be found in this book, *Skillful Futures*. Parents and children can experience learning together through shared experiences and practical hands-on enjoyment."

– Deborah Sandoval, Middle School Counselor

"Children are naturally curious about how the world works. Those with opportunities to explore changing future economies and industries and experiment, build, and connect to real-world experiences with guidance and support, will be best poised to meet the needs of our rapidly changing future economy and industries."

– Erica Cox, Teacher of the Year

Skillful Futures offers practical guidance for parents and educators for how to prepare children to engage in experiences to further their opportunities in choosing a career. In the changing climate of careers in the 21st century, Ms. Morgan looks at various ways in which children can prosper within an educational setting that will meet the individual needs of a child to prepare them for various careers. This is a must-read for any parent with school-aged children."

– Lisa Gill, Teacher of the Year

"As a twenty-year veteran elementary teacher, I wholeheartedly recommend parents read *Skillful Futures*. I totally connected with the thinking and experiences suggested in this book as ways for parents to support their children's future. As we move to an ever-evolving job market, this is a must-read not only for parents but educators alike!"

– April Marie Sheffield, Elementary Teacher

"Many thanks to Oceanside Schools for your kind coins that supported "Kids for Peace" in raising money for building a complete Kids for Peace School for the orphaned and vulnerable children of western Kenya. Reiko Kenya, a nonprofit organization, particularly thanks Phyllis T. Morgan for volunteering her chess skills and teaching our middle school students this valuable game, and for coordination with the Career Tech (CTE) nursing classes from Oceanside High, who raised funds to build our health office at the school, as well as the Palmquist school students for their interest in gardening and bringing the science of *hügelkultur* (centuries-old raised garden concept using debris to compost raised garden beds) to create our Peace Garden. We wholeheartedly thank the American children for building and equipping our Kids for Peace School."

– Edward Ochenge Kabaka, Executive Director at Reiko, Kenya, and Former Chief Officer for Public Service Management and Administration Kenya

SKILLFUL FUTURES

The Strategic Guide to Parenting Kids for Career Success

PHYLLIS T. MORGAN

Skillful Futures: The Strategic Guide to Parenting Kids for Career Success
Published by Moonscape Press
San Diego, California, U.S.A.

MORGAN, PHYLLIS T., Author
SKILLFUL FUTURES
PHYLLIS T. MORGAN

Library of Congress Control Number: 2023904212

ISBN: 978-1-7366717-5-7, 978-1-7366717-8-8 (paperback)
ISBN: 978-1-7366717-7-1 (hardcover)
ISBN: 978-1-7366717-6-4 (digital)

EDUCATION / Parent Participation
FAMILY & RELATIONSHIPS / Education
REFERENCE / Personal & Practical Guides

Editing: Tiffany Vakilian (tiffanyvakilian.com)
Editing: Lisa Shrewsberry (getfinelines.weebly.com)
Book Design: Michelle M. White (mmwbooks.com)
Publishing Management: Susie Schaefer (finishthebookpublishing.com)

QUANTITY PURCHASES:
Schools, companies, professional groups, clubs, and other organizations
may qualify for special terms when ordering quantities of this title.
For information, email phyllis.moonscapepress@gmail.com

This book is printed in the United States of America.

*To my two beautiful sons
and my six wonderful grandchildren for whom
I continue to endeavor to create learning experiences.*

*To the many teachers I have worked with
who taught me so much, and to all the thousands of students
who taught me even more about how they learn.*

CREATING SKILLFUL LEARNING EXPERIENCES FOR CHILDREN PRESCHOOL TO CAREERS

The following insights and views are based on observations of a visionary award-winning educator with fifty years experience who stresses that there is a current need for parents to 'jump in' and help create many early learning experiences around life skills with their children. Transferable and adaptable skills will be critical to cope with flexible industry changes in their child's future.

> "Tell me, and I will forget.
> Show me, and I will see.
> Teach me, and I will remember.
> Engage me, and I will learn.
> 'Experience', and I will never forget."
> – *Benjamin Franklin*

We may not have a crystal ball to help us with future careers, but if we look at the signs around us, we can see that many transferable skills will be a key to success.

Whether we play a game or go to school we should be aware of the ultimate purpose of why we are engaged in the process of learning.

TABLE OF CONTENTS

Introduction

> *"When we educate, we educate the whole child."*
>
> ~ NEA (National Teachers Association), ACSA (Association of California School Administrators), PTA (Parent Teacher Association)

The pendulum has swung.

While for over twenty-years our eyes focused on bachelor's degrees to earn **high paying** jobs, we inadvertently created an over-abundance of non-certified workers. Many young college students took "College for All" to focus on Liberal Arts studies with no industry connection. Those who graduated were not certified to do any specific work and needed to return to community colleges or technical schools for more training.

In the meantime, our high schools lost many of their hands-on trade courses. Introductory experiences into carpentry, mechanics, and electrical trades literally disappeared from curriculum spreadsheets, and so have the skilled workers. Today, a certified plumber, electrician, or engine mechanic can easily demand over six figures. But education systems created their own monster — a community of students in debt who are trying to catch up with whatever industry they can prepare for quickly.

In 2020, we gained a generation of X and Z children deeply affected by a worldwide pandemic. Currently, about two-thirds of our students have lost a year (perhaps two) of school and learning. Schools are focusing on basic catch-up — as they should — but they are losing the interest of students who have been entertained on digital devices. Engaging students is the name of the game. And the interest level had better be high or you will lose them.

I began this book with the purpose of helping parents respond to post-pandemic learning. Families needed to design educational opportunities out of thin air. However, as I began writing this manuscript, it became evident to me that the gaps were far greater than we imagined. The shift that public school education needs to make is far outside the box of setting up business as usual. Children who were used to finding entertainment on devices were not interested in returning to traditional formal schoolwork at all. Teachers shared how difficult it was now to channel students into subjects that no longer interested or applied to them. Many new disruptive and non-attentive behaviors came through the doors of the schools, as well as ever-increasing absentee rates, creating challenging situations for teachers, and many chose to retire. We see serious gaps in learning where students are missing the meaning behind the reason for why we learn.

I spent time at a middle school in 2022, teaching ancient history to hundreds of students. We drew grid cities replicating ancient civilizations, north to south and east to west.

"Miss, what's a centimeter?" a student asked. "What do you mean when you say I need to walk three blocks to the next canal in Mohenjo Daro? What's a block?"

One student needing to sign out to go to the bathroom looked at the round analog clock on the wall. They asked the teacher, "What time is it? I don't know how to read that kind of clock."

Over the past two years, close to twenty percent of the students at that middle school didn't "attend school" in any form, whether via physical campus attendance or Distance Learning. I know because I experienced their teaching as a long-term substitute. Many students would log into attendance, stay on for a short while, then disappear for the rest of the class.

When students begin middle school, we often lose their attention for a variety of reasons, but to keep them going, we need to pull them into the **purpose** and the **why** for coming.

Based on my experience, middle school has usually been ground zero for missed opportunities. Most European schools introduce skilled experiences for their students in middle school. Students go from imagining work as they did in elementary schools to doing work that they all can use at home to further develop for industry or side-hustles. It now makes perfect sense to bring back the engaging, hands-on trade experiences that will also create successful futures here in American schools as early as possible. Middle school is the perfect time to expose students to as many skills as they can learn. The groundwork for **why** we go to school needs to be established at this time.

By middle school, students need to be exposed to many hands-on skills that are not only engaging their interest but can be useful in all stages of life. You may ask yourself, "Why is there a growing need to begin in middle school and not in high school and college?" Here's the reason: this three-year period is critical if you want to grab the attention of the young for them to develop multiple skills and talents. Unfortunately, it is often a missed opportunity for learning about how school relates to the work world.

Traditionally, this is also the time when parents place their children in sports programs or dance classes to hold their interest. Children can only dream of being a sports hero, an actress, or a dancer. There is no exposure to any skilled jobs experiences that will develop other interest and imaginations for an A-to-Z plan to back up ways to live out their dreams. As a parent, you might spend thousands of dollars on multiple theme park experiences but are not providing fun ways to teach children abilities such as culinary skills, harvesting, preparing, and bringing food to the table. Simple experiences of having children open a kitchen drawer filled with utensils and naming them and showing how they are used — you know, the skills of life — are learning experiences. Others include taking the time to teach your children how to scramble eggs, make a batch of cookies, clean their own clothes, fold them, and design and organize areas where they can find everything in their room, create and keep a budget...these practical everyday life skills will build resilient children, and they are not skills typically taught in schools.

If we look for **skilled workers** such as electricians, carpenters, plumbers, or mechanics, they are difficult to find when you need one. There are so few of them and, based on demand, they can pick and choose their jobs based on the largest jobs that garner the most income.

You may be waiting forever to find someone to fix that little leak. But the student who goes to community college/trade school and becomes licensed in a trade can work their way up to a six-figure income in **less than two years.**

Skilled tradesmen, once revered in ancient times, should be revered once again as essential workers for every community. Just recently, a radio news station celebrated a company set up by seventeen-year-old girls from a local high school. They had all taken a course in mechanics and decided to earn money by changing the oil in cars and working on carburetors from one of the family garages. One girl said, "Well, we learned a skill this year and we turned it into a lucrative business." The radio station was focusing on young female businesses, but I saw it more about finding ways to make money using practical skills.

In the 21st century it helps to be a Jack/Jill of all trades.

Today, community college costs are minimal to attend as compared to four-year universities. Our country has supplied funding to realize the goal of a free or affordable public K-14 system. Any student who isn't certain what they really want to do for a career can train and have a skill they will have for life to make or supplement an income. The need for skilled workers is *so* great that local trade businesses are saying, "Just tell any high school graduate to apply and come into the business ready to learn, we'll teach them everything they need. The only thing they'll need to do is invest in their own tools along the way."

I was aware of the studies over the years showing students with a two-year gap in their education would find it hard to catch up. Students who are that far behind may just drop out. But we can't allow our children to lose their ability to be self-sufficient. Engaging them with purpose, interest, and hands-on learning is key to creating independent, gainfully employed adults. It is paramount to create an early expectation around the "why" we go to school. There needs to be an educational shift in American schools, but this starts in the American home.

Throughout this book, I hope to share with you many of the techniques used by my colleagues, myself, and schools to create life-long learners. It has become increasingly evident that tomorrow's world will need students who are equipped to learn many skills on their own.

In keeping with the idea of engagement, I am taking the liberty of introducing each chapter of this book with some insight from others about the game of chess in the hope that I might also engage you and win you over to introducing this ancient analytical game to your children. It is a perfect time to bring out a hands-on game and give children a chance to get off their devices. I have often been asked how I managed to survive so many years as a principal.

My answer was always the same: "I know how to play chess."

Purpose

What Does an Involved Parent Look Like in the 21st Century World?

"By five years of age a child's brain is 90 percent developed; don't waste the opportunity to teach them everything they are hungry to learn."

~ Arizona State University Study

There is a growing need for parents to be very involved in guiding their children's learning, especially now and into the future. If the Pandemic has taught us anything it is that there is a struggle for many children to get back on track and the ability for schools to create the enormity of skills children will need to adapt to changing future jobs.

It is a time in which children need to learn skills. Many parents haven't been exposed to building or renovating furniture themselves, but it is the perfect opportunity to learn along with our children how to build a shed or a playhouse or put together a picnic table or a birdhouse using a YouTube video. Create opportunities for opening the toolbox, naming, and using the tools and knowing when to use them.

Most parents understand the need to schedule swimming lessons for their children during the summer, recognizing this one skill might save their child's life. But in so many ways, every skill your child can acquire in their early years might very well be the key to providing a future job. You can't learn too many skills for adapting to future needs. Industries will change often, and so will the skills that employees will need — hence, the need for transferable skills.

If statistics are suggesting that most children will have at least twelve different jobs in their future, a child might choose one certified job and find they hate it and want to pursue their interest in another skilled profession that they began learning earlier. (Today you are no longer stuck in one industry for life unless the opportunities are there, and you choose to stay.) Many will grow outside businesses, a side business (a hustle) because of their native ability to use the internet.

As a former principal, I found many parents still asking advice or seeking reassurance about their children's goals for the future. Just last June, a parent shared, "My son just informed me on his graduation day that he is *not* going to college as we had guided him to do. We've saved the money for *years*, and we kept him talking about where he wanted to go to university. We even traveled last year to look at all the campuses where he had an interest."

"So, what does he have in mind for his future?" I asked.

"He tells me he wants to learn to be a car mechanic!" the upset mother cried out.

"That's great!" I said. "Tell him to learn all he can but then turn his trade into working as a boat mechanic. There are over ten thousand boats sitting in San Diego Bay and there are *no* mechanics. Boats are literally rotting in their slips. Beginning licensed mechanics start at $80 an hour."

"What?! Is that true?" she asked, suddenly interested.

"Absolutely! We have at least a 20-year gap since mechanics were last trained. All the older mechanics are retiring and there is no one to train the new ones. By the way, where is your son going for his training?"

As our conversation continued, the parent revealed that her son was planning on going to a local community college offering a diesel mechanics program. I encouraged her saying that her son wasn't ready to return to traditional classroom learning and that this was more than okay. He was eager to learn a skill that he could always use, a hands-on trade. I reminded her that tradesmen are some of the highest paid and revered people in society. Society can't work without them, and we have created a scarcity! You can't have too many skills for providing services for yourself or others.

"You have a point, but I wanted more for him," she said, still doubting.

"College can always be there, the funds are there, and he knows it, but he is focusing on something that interests him and will serve his interest now. Don't you see? *It's a win-win*. He learns a trade, something he can always use, and perhaps it leads to something else, perhaps becoming an engineer. He will still have finished two years of transferable college credits and he has a trade to help him out whenever he wants to make money."

She admitted that, whether she agreed with his decision or not, there wasn't much she could do about it. It was his decision.

"It's all good. He's not dropping out of life," I reminded her. "He's engaging in it, and he's excited by it." Her son was not alone in his decision to choose another path. Many students going into college are not ready and are taking a gap year (a year off school) because they just have no idea what they want to do. For those parents, I advise them to make sure their child is earning a wage and learning to pay their way, not just sitting in their bedrooms playing video games.

There is so much that parents, like this one, can be aware of earlier in their child's education that can lead them to a fulfilling and lucrative career outside of college. At least by middle school, students need experiences with trades and shadowing opportunities, way before they even get into high school.

Parents need to know that by the time they get to high school, their child is supposed to select an industry pathway for which they are provided elective courses in the field they want to get certified. Those electives are called *articulated courses* and earn the students' college credits. Keep me posted on how he's doing. Believe me, I need a good mechanic. Tell him I will be ready to hire him as soon as he gets certified."

ENGAGE

To *engage* students is to make them: Enthusiastic, involved, absorbed, engrossed, or enthralled.

"Okay, stop fighting over whose car belongs to whom. Let's sort the cars into colors and race the red against the blues, and the oranges against the greens. Ready, go, let's sort," said the mother to her two sons who had been sitting in the corner of the bedroom with a box filled with dozens of cars throwing them at each other.

1

How Do We First Learn?

"In chess the small one can become the big one,"

~ GLORIA IN THE MOVIE *QUEEN OF KATWE*

---

*S*ad is the home without expectations.

As parents, we need to voice clear expectations. That way, when our children become adults, they will be expected to become independent, self-sufficient individuals who create their own happiness and share it with others.

If you are reading this book, you are already an "active" parent looking for ways to help your child become successful at school and in life. Parents of school age students will appreciate this because this book includes early learning strategies (tips and tricks used by many teachers) that will help create the foundational learning for more advanced learning to follow.

From the beginning of time, you have heard that parents are the child's first teachers. Today, the parent is the child's main teacher and perhaps many of you are recognizing you may be your child's best teacher. Research states that in the 21st century the average adult will have over a dozen jobs. As I write this, professionals in the college arena are telling me this number is conservative. Traditional schools are slow to adapt and change. It will be up to the parents to find or provide the opportunities.

What could cause this shift? Many things, but certainly a worldwide pandemic has created the opportunity for parents to reconnect with their children. Has it always been this way? I believe some parents have relegated teaching to schools, but have forgotten that they are their child's most important teacher. They have succumbed to a systematic way of thinking.

Parents need to truly understand their role; this is not the time for business as usual. The Pandemic and the digital world have changed the playing field for everyone. For many in past generations, parents taught children some basic skills as they entered school such as the alphabet and counting to thirty. Then, they would drop their children at the front door of a school hoping the school would meet their children at whatever level and teach the rest.

During the Pandemic, to meet the need for equal educational opportunities for all learning remotely, almost overnight every child received a computer and internet access. The twenty-year-old textbook that is still supplied for check out in many schools is lacking current or accurate information or even a relatable syllabus that creates a relationship from past lives to developing future lives. So, I ask you, what skills are you providing for your children's future success? What I'm seeing is much of the same — parents have learned to provide the *same way* as they were taught from their homes.

Nobody knows how your child can access information better than you. You know exactly what they can do and what they are ready to learn. When a teacher meets your child for the first time, they need to figure all that out. They need to ask themselves: *Where are the gaps and where are the connections?* Now, imagine your child walking into a classroom of twenty or thirty children, all at different levels. It certainly gives you a new appreciation for the scope of what teachers need to do to help everyone be successful. It takes close to a month of schooling for teachers to get one-on-one with every child to understand exactly what they already know and figure out their personality and learning style. When your child begins Kindergarten, you can supply a teacher with a short narrative of what you've experienced with your child's learning such as: "Kevin and I read two books a night. He reads me the first sentence and then I read to him the rest. He practices writing words and can write his full name. He can recognize and count to one hundred and we play math games mainly with addition."

From the day your children were born, they watched your every move, listened to your voice, memorized your facial expressions, watched the shape of your mouth to learn to speak, and used every one of their senses to explore the world around them. Small children have an avid curiosity for learning. They are trying to figure out their world and how they are going to maneuver within it. It is the optimum time to teach them. You need to grab every opportunity to connect and engage their attention beyond two minutes and to take the time to do this early.

Research published on the internet states that close to 65 percent of the human population are visual learners. That means if you show me how to do it or draw pictures or charts of what I need to know, I will learn it faster and process it better than seeing it in text or hearing the information told to me. It may surprise parents to know younger children are closer to 80 percent visual learners. Children learn by mimicking. They are wired that way. When babies watch you perform a simple task, they instinctively use their visual learning skills to replicate that task.

Once they successfully perform the task, they want to do it over and over again (repetition) to make sure they have it. As a teacher, I recognized that it takes children constant repetition to make the patterns stick. Research says it takes the average adult at least 16 repeated sequences to make any memory or behavior automatic. Just try learning the sequence of any new device, a car, a phone, a new computer, and you'll realize it takes constant repetition, time, and patience.

Presently, the standard for College and Career Readiness is that *all* students need to be reading independently at a third-grade level by the third grade to continue with the pace in schools. There is extensive research behind this statement. Students up to third grade are still learning to read, however, after grade three they are expected to independently read informational text — they should be reading to learn. Years of government data found that students who dropped out of high school were never able to catch up.

The state of Mississippi, which had repeatedly held the lowest reading scores in the United States based on standardized tests, decided to 'take another tack' for creating a partnership with parents and educators to focus on the importance of reading. They created the Literacy-Based Promotion Act in 2013 which requires all third-graders pass a reading test before moving to fourth grade. By 2019, students in Mississippi's grade four had some of the highest scores in the nation, proving once again the schools cannot do it alone.

> *The standard measurement for college and career readiness is that all students can read independently at a third-grade level by third grade.*

It makes sense to teach children when they are ready and eager to learn. You can see that an average three-year-old has developed enough of an attention span and fundamental skills to learn symbols and names. At three, a child's attention span is close to eight minutes for learning a single step process. Patterns are part of a child's language and math acquisition. Besides reading stories to children each day, playing with puzzles or sequencing blocks by size, shape and color are also a great start. I sat down with a group of toddlers grabbing and hollering about which blocks were theirs. I dumped all the blocks in the middle and told them we were going to play a game, but we needed to take turns. Then, I observed what happened.

Games have rules. I shared with the children they would miss a turn if they didn't follow the rules. We went clockwise, and a little girl went first. I told her to pick a color. She picked pink. I told her she was only to pick the pink ones, but we were going to line them up from biggest to smallest.

She went to the pile, examined all the blocks, and picked the biggest pink block. This simple game took a good fifteen minutes, which tested the limits of a preschool student, because **as a rule, a child's attention span increases by five minutes for each year as they become older.** During that time, adding simple rules taught the little girl and others how to play, sort, and take turns. The bonus was it taught them how to analyze the pile of blocks and then sort by size. Any time you can turn an exercise into an activity that requires **analytical skills**, you have gained a transferable skill that can be used into their future. The group of children understood all those concepts at three years old.

A word about dyslexia: this may be one of the first symptoms you may find in some children who are having difficulty learning sequencing and patterns in early childhood. There are varying degrees of dyslexia from mild to moderate to severe. It is *so* common, in fact, that many states do not even test for it as a disability. One out of five students may experience some early delays such as dyslexia, which becomes detectable when a child reaches three or four years of age.

Many parents have thought by placing their child in a school or preschool these delays could be instantly recognized or cured. It doesn't work that way (schools can assist with disabilities but they can't cure them). This is where observing, engaging in play, and learning about your children comes in.

Children need a lot of repetition, one-on-one instruction, and many opportunities to make connections to catch up by third grade, and third grade levels are crucial to reach as a benchmark for future years. All children are different, however. As a parent, pay attention to what strategies are introduced to your child at school so you can repeat them at home.

2

Communication

"Life is a game of chess changing with each move."

~ CHINESE PROVERB

Developing **communication skills** is one of the main reasons why education needs to start earlier than formal school years in children's lives, especially when it comes to recognizing letter symbols, letter sounds, and writing letters as part of a child's daily activity. If we expect children to be reading and writing fluently by third grade, then it makes perfect sense to give them time to access those experiences earlier.

Language Arts in schools include fluent reading, writing, listening, and speaking skills. Obviously, young children first learn to communicate through speaking. By the age of two, your child will have picked up enough essential vocabulary to point out objects they recognize and say their names back to you.

There are many ways to increase a child's vocabulary by exposing them to childhood stories, rhyming songs, sharing pictures, sign language games, and simply communicating with them often. The more communication you have between you and your child the more they pick up vocabulary. It might surprise you that the average student who enters school at the age of five has over ten thousand words in their vocabulary pool! If English is a second language for your child, you may want to expose your child often to English vocabulary so that they can transition easily into public schools that teach only in English.

"I don't want to go to school," yelled the four-year-old boy to his mother.

"Why?"

"Everyone can read books and I can't."

"That's okay. We all learn differently, you'll catch up. We'll practice every night, you'll see."

"No, I won't, it's too hard."

"Everything is hard at first until you learn how to do it. Then it becomes easy."

"Why do I have to go to school anyway?"

"We all keep learning new things for the rest of our lives. I already need to go back to school to learn new ways to do things for work."

"You need to encourage me."

"So, what does the word encourage mean?" asked the mother.

The boy throws both his arms in the air and says, "How am I supposed to know what it means?"

"See? That is why we go to school."

Creating daily activities and games using an alphabet chart can develop reading patterns. An easy one is having a child start by standing on a line, then allowing the child to run up to an alphabet chart on the wall and touch the letter, calling the letter by name, and running back to the starting line. They can receive a tally mark for each correct answer. This also allows the child to move which (going back to age and attention span) is critical for engagement at this stage.

It is valuable to have picture cards or picture puzzles for children to play with to build vocabulary and match the letter that identifies the initial letter sound, such as placing a (B) next to the picture of a Bird.

At four years old, a child should be writing the letters as well. By five, they should be making the sound and writing three letters at a time. Eventually, this will lead to three letter words such as dog and cat.

Communication is one of the **essential skill elements** in today's fast-moving world. So is daily communication. By the age of three, the average child can speak to you in a simple sentence or phrase, not just one-word demands. On average, a three-year-old has a vocabulary of over a thousand words.

A quick activity you can do at home is to check for understanding. You can have your children repeat back a one-step instruction, and then later repeat two-step instructions to check auditory processing. Here's an example:

"John, can you put the ketchup in the refrigerator? John, can you tell me what I asked you to do?" As this repetition becomes successful, ask John to put back the ketchup and bring you a bottle of water. This simple check of processing is valuable for checking other delays in language acquisition.

Children up to the third grade are learning to read. After third grade, they are reading to learn.

Most of the essential skills we need to focus on with children go back to the old school of three 'R's", reading, writing, and 'rithmetic (or arithmetic), better known as mathematics. Young children need to first verbalize their understanding, then this becomes the foundation for these core areas of learning. Working on daily communication is essential.

To encourage competency in communication, by the age of three, begin by having your child try to speak to you in sentences. A young child's self-esteem often becomes vulnerable in the early years. In a first-grade class, for instance, when children see other children reading books, understanding the text, and writing, they often feel defeated if they can't do the same. This is when children need to be taught to understand that everyone is different, and everyone learns at their own pace. Encourage them and explain that this doesn't mean they are not smart.

Children need to understand how to measure their own learning and measure their own growth. *Success breeds more success.*

If your child is experiencing early delays, consider seeking outside tutoring or even home school support until your child can manage to keep up independently. Give your child a chance to experience success. *Young children begin to give up and not try when they see others able to do things they can't.*

3

Creating a Home Learning Environment

"Chess is played with the mind and not with the hands."

~ RENAUD AND KAHN

As an educational consultant, I was asked to help set up successful educational environments in the most challenging of circumstances during the Pandemic. I remember I needed to help a single mother with four children set up a 1000 square foot condominium to accommodate multiple learning experiences.

The mother had two boys who were preschoolers — one who was almost four and one who was almost five. She also had a six-year-old girl and a seven-year-old boy. Clearly, she had her hands full. I was happy to help.

The condo had two bedrooms, two baths, a living room, and a small dining table in the kitchen. She had a desk in her bedroom which she was using for her office as she was asked to perform her duties as a digital marketer at home. She told me she was expected to put in about seven hours online per day.

I could see how stressed she was with having to monitor her daughter and son's virtual distance learning and keep her very active preschool children busy, learning, and away from the older children learning on

Zoom. I shared with her that in most schools four hours of scheduled time is spent around basics, but the rest is filled with recess, lunch, PE, library, and hopefully some social studies and science which can be integrated into language arts and mathematics as themes. **Integrated learning produces a lot of cross subject connection.**

I suggested we needed to look at the set-ups we had in the house to best construct work environments. I shared with her that workspaces today in industry and in many of today's classrooms offer spaces for various activities such as soft chairs, couches for reading, work group tables, single desks, and even outdoor settings. **When you think about it, we always have to get up and move about our environment to refresh our thoughts.** Even our smart watches tell us to get up and move. Since the mom lived on the ground floor, she had an extended patio with a picnic table that could be used for recess breaks and art activities for the children to do together.

She shared that her industry didn't care when her work projects were completed: it was more of a weekly deadline. I suggested that she could get up very early and put in a few hours of work before everyone got up and put in the remaining hours after eight when the family would have dinner, their baths, and were in bed. The good news is mom still had a sustainable job, and she could possibly pay for some added adult support.

We talked more about the environment. The boys all slept in one bedroom. There was a bunk bed and another single bed against another wall. If she bought one small play table and four chairs for that bedroom, she could have a work area for the preschool boys. There was a lot of wall space with posters, and I thought we could create a cork wall for hanging up alphabet charts, number charts, and, perhaps, a little whiteboard for modeling examples. We could also tack up samples of their work projects on the board along with the learning schedule. For the two school-age children, I suggested the basic workspace should be the kitchen table. I suggested that the little girl sit at one end of the table and her brother at the other end to give everyone their space.

The mom shared that the little girl (age six) seemed sharper than her little boy (age seven). I told her this was not uncommon. Girls in the early years often mature faster than boys.

I added that this was an advantage when we shared educational games; both would be in-sync with playing certain games together. (Scientists at Newcastle University in the U.K. have discovered that girls tend to optimize brain connections earlier than boys.) She agreed, "That is so true, no matter what, she wants to beat him at everything." She described something that was not unusual. It is why I introduced the earning system. It isn't about winning and making someone else lose; it is about earning a penny for your own bank. (See Chapter 7 on Earning Power).

So, we worked on their schedules, building in recess time for all four children to avoid the mom giving herself more work than would be necessary for the children's learning. The schedule sounded like a lot at first, but if parents stick to it and keep earning charts while paying real money for chores, expectations, and work products, along with implementing fines (consequences), the entire system will become increasingly easier to manage. **The key to everything is to BE CONSISTENT.** Consistency sets up an atmosphere of fairness and everyone gets on the same page for what is expected. Just always go to the reward and fine charts that are posted on the refrigerator. (You can add to or take off expectations any time there is a need.) For instance, one day one of the boys threw a ball at his brother in the living room and it shattered a picture frame. Mom went over to the chart and wrote "we don't throw anything at anyone inside the house or there will be a fine of 25 cents."

Always consistently reward, and fine just as consistently. Don't let your child pull you into a negotiation with, "He hit me first." You can ask the other child if he did it or if anyone saw him do it. If no one agrees, he gets the fine for hitting; if they did see the other hit first, both get fined. This is the action of *tough love* — being fair, consistent, and quick. It helps move everything forward when boundaries are set. Children respect boundaries because someone needs to draw a picture of what safety looks like in the home. ***Children don't learn if they don't feel safe.*** There always needs to be someone in charge of enforcing the boundaries. In the house, it should be the parent or supervising adult at home who is in charge. If there are two parents taking charge, **everyone needs to get on the same page with the expectations and the delivery of rewards and consequences.**

Our public schools centered all rules around the Three Bs: Be Responsible, Be Respectful, Be Safe. Believe me, as a principal, there wasn't a single incident that occurred when I couldn't ask a young child which of the three principles they violated.

> *Boundaries and their consistent enforcement are the keys to fairness.*

When two children have a disagreement, they can all learn rock-paper-scissors. The winner of three tries wins. This quick exercise allows children who are disagreeing over the smallest events on playgrounds or in the home to settle their own disputes quickly and move on. There must be consequences for certain behaviors. Hitting someone breaks the "Be Respectful" rule, so there should be a fine. Every specific action can create a callback to the one of the Three Bs.

"Did you finish the work before the snack? Is that being responsible?"

"Did you just jump off the top of the bunk bed? Is that being safe?"

On the playground, using the rock-paper-scissors option can go something like this:

"He was over the line. It didn't count."

"If you can't agree then do rock-paper-scissors and the best out of three tries gets the point."

Empowering children to settle simple disputes teaches them to find solutions as a consistent and clear strategy to move on without calling on a parent, a teacher, or a judge to determine everything for them.

4

Schedules and Routines

"Chess is an entire world of just 64 squares.
I feel safe in it. I can control it. I can dominate it.
And it's predictable.
So, if I get hurt I only have myself to blame."

~ Beth Harmon, *The Queen's Gambit*

Consistency sets up an atmosphere of fairness so everyone can get on the same page for what is expected. One of the best frameworks for consistency is a schedule. Below is a home learning schedule that can be adapted for after-school or even weekend time.

The trick to a learning schedule is to focus on the basics first. Language Arts and Mathematics should be addressed in the morning. Children concentrate better earlier, when their brains are rested and energized.

A Sample Home Learning Schedule

8:00 **Breakfast:** a snack or meal preferably with protein (the brain is a muscle that needs protein: egg, peanut butter toast, protein shake.)

8:30 Create a **mindset** around this week's central theme. Identify an objective of the day by answering the question, "What are we going to learn today?"

8:45 *Blazing Pencils: Have children write as much as they can about anything.

(Preschoolers just letters for two minutes, Kindergarten words for two minutes, first grade and up write to five minutes and write in sentences.) **Like brushing your teeth each day, this one exercise will create fluent writers over time.**

Count the number of letters or words and see if the child beat yesterday's total. Have them read their entry to one other if you're working with more than one child.

9:00 **Language Arts:** Lessons can be thematically designed (reading, social studies, or science themes are often used). Grade Level Standards for Common Core Reading, Writing, Listening and Speaking materials can be found or purchased online, or distributed through Public Charter School enrollment, or whichever school your children are enrolled in.

10:30 **Recess:** nutritious snack and free play time.

11:00 **Mathematics:** Lessons designed around State Grade Level Standards (which can be found on the State Department of Education's website in most states), tie in some problem solving and creative thinking.

*Draw an Array (third grade and up — make an arrangement of numbers or number problems in rows and columns and spend five minutes filling in the six through nine times tables.) This little exercise completed each day gives children practice, helps them understand the repeated patterns, and creates a tool to check answers during computation exercises.

12:30 **Lunch** and free-play games or get in a run.

1:45 **Reading:** silent reading (30 minutes) grades two and up, or an adult reading aloud.

To make sure your child's body is ready to tackle a consistent schedule, nutritionists share a good rule of thumb: always have protein in a breakfast meal. Nutritionists have shared that our brain is a muscle. For children to be able to concentrate, they need high protein, low carb, low sugar meals for their brains to function properly. Some breakfast suggestions fitting these criteria might include a protein smoothie, an egg, or toast with peanut butter.

Several activities can start at the table, after the dishes are cleared. "Blazing Pencils" is my personal favorite. It is a quick writing activity using a timer set for two to five minutes. The preschool children sit for two minutes, writing as many letters as they can, and the six- and seven-year-olds write what they want to share today for five minutes.

A "flashlight" is a collection of small index cards on a chrome ring used to build up sight words or collect new vocabulary.

(Quick ideas for writing might be to tell something fun you did yesterday or something you want to do today.) After the timer goes off, they count the total number of words or letters they wrote today, and they try to beat the number from the day before. This quick activity each day will build writing fluency over time. Encourage older children to read aloud what they wrote. By 9:00 a.m., the school-age children will probably be logging into their Zoom or other internet lesson with their earbuds.

This is the time to play language arts games with preschoolers. You may want to go over letters and sounds, and write the letters for building fluency with sight words such as: the, of, that, through (sight words are words that are transitional in a sentence usually not specific nouns, adjectives, or specific verbs). When children can say the word just by recognizing the sight words, they can help the student read a sentence more fluently, which then helps the child understand the passage better. These can be identified and reviewed daily using index cards.

Fluency is reading without stopping. It's the key for building comprehension when you begin reading. You will be amazed how fast kids pick up on the sight words with a little earning power. One of the tricks many of our schools' teachers used was a large ring they called a "flashlight." Whenever a child did not know a sight word, the child would make a small size index card, punch a hole, and put the word on the ring. After a child reads and recognizes the word ten times, they can take the card off the ring. Children could see their ring stack getting smaller and knew they were having success with learning all the words.

Following the suggested scheduling, hands-on activities are necessary to break up the direct teaching time. Puzzles are good. Pull out up to four puzzles for preschoolers — one could be the alphabet, one for numbers, and perhaps some picture puzzles that can enhance analytical skills. You can set a timer and have your child try all four puzzles and earn some pennies, or whatever reward system you prefer when they complete their work. A little motivation can incentivize most task completion.

After an outdoor recess break, it is time for mathematics. After some guided practice, with independent math computation completed, it is time for lunch. This is a great time for everyone to eat together.

If it is a nice day, children can have a picnic in the park, and everyone goes for a "run for fun" around the park a few times for aerobic exercise. Tallies can be used to calculate how many laps equal a mile, reinforcing more math concepts.

Older children can often calculate four or five laps around a track equals one mile (again, they are experiencing the value of numbers through measurement.) Many teachers use the United States map in a program called "Run Across America" which tracks miles and converts them to distance equivalencies for running across America. Home school children can track their miles and keep the map up for years to see how long it took them to run across the United States. Over time, they can calculate how many miles they run in a week, averaging their distance and estimating how many weeks or months it will take to cross the continent. Older children can also learn the names of states and capitals as they travel across America or cities and towns and research places of interest and create a travel brochure of places they want to see in the future.

After a return from outside play, it is always a good time to settle down to reading. First and second grade students can easily go off in a corner to read quietly for twenty or thirty minutes or they can practice reading several books out loud to each other. While they read independently, you can read a simple story book or two to any preschoolers in your household.

For comprehension, it is good for everyone to take turns and share a little about what they read afterward. Always have children share the title and author and the main characters, the setting, and what happened. You can follow up with a question or two like: was there a problem, was there a lesson to be learned, or was there a moral to this story?

After silent reading and review, it is again time for some hands-on activity. You and the children may have selected something on *Pinterest* or *Mystery Science* to construct or replicate that align to a theme developed for the week. Theming is a good way to start each week. Consider topics such as magnetism, shapes of leaves, or fairy tales. As much as you can, include a project that will be completed in a week. For instance, make a chart where you glue down the leaves collected in a week, describe the shape and size, and the type of tree they fell from.

Try to include at least one or two art, math, and science activities in each project. If you include measurement in a project such as measuring the length of a leaf, have the children measure in inches and turn the ruler around and measure it in centimeters. Children need a lot of experience with measuring using both metric and Imperial systems (which the USA still uses). They also need to understand that the leaf may be two inches long, but it is also over five centimeters and the values are the same when discussing length.

Each child may want to choose which one activity they do each day. Giving children a **choice** of a couple of activities gets a lot more buy-in from them than telling them what they have to do every day and every moment. "Do you want to make the origami rabbit today or do the chemical change experiment?"

Perhaps your children are making origami rabbits for Easter. When they finish the rabbit, have them unfold it into a flat piece of paper called a **net**. Then have your child name all the geometric shapes it created by tracing the folds (the older children can also take a ruler and measure the sides of each triangle in inches then centimeters).

When doing chemical experiments for science, always have children put on a pair of safety glasses and measure the liquids and weigh the powders before they observe the reaction. Lab safety isn't just something students cover in high school! If you really want smaller children to feel like a real scientist, purchase a little lab coat online and have them wear it when they work on science projects. *Voila!* You have a future scientist.

If you know your six through nine times tables, you will know most of the times tables. There are at least 150 sight words for building fluency in 1st grade. (see frequently used word list researched by Fry and Dolch.)

As a principal of a STEM (science, technology, engineering, and math) school, I observed students wearing white lab coats whenever they were doing experiments that involved measurement. We had an outdoor organic garden at the rear of the school. Each day's harvest had to be weighed and packaged with a designated price. The garden fund made $1.00 for every two pounds we grew in our garden, which we then in turn sold back to the school's cafeteria to serve in our school's salad bar for lunch or sold to local restaurants.

Children love to experience playing like they are working at a real job. In the garden they were sometimes the scientist, sometimes the shopkeeper to figure out how much the cafeteria manager owed the garden fund or the chef who uses a recipe to create meals from the vegetables that were harvested.

Whenever you are doing any type of experiment or construction it is good to wonder out loud what type of a job a person does if they do this type of work. Young children love to imagine themselves in a job. For instance, you can explain that biochemists often perform chemical changes each day when trying to discover new ways to treat diseases. Intermediate school students (grades 3-5) can research the different types of biochemists that are out there, they can check how much they earn, and what local industries they work for. This is also a perfect time to discover who does what in the world. **Pathful or Nepris jobs** are great internet sites to listen to people who actually work in a field and find out how they chose that line of work and how much they earn (See **Resources** for URLs). Listening to someone's journey into their career is always interesting. You discover that many scientists found their careers by accident. They just loved science, took a job in the industry, and worked their way up the ladder when they saw themselves wanting to learn more. Helping children make these kinds of connections to real jobs and the work world is part of developing their skillful futures!

After everyone cleans up after the afternoon activity, give children free choice. They can play outside, inside, or perhaps entertain themselves with a device game for thirty minutes.

This will give mom or dad a break to make phone calls or complete other daily tasks for themselves. Children could have free play and choice, as long as it is done quietly.

Before or after dinner can be a fun exercise time. Maybe your family likes to hike, play hide-and-seek in the park, go to the beach, or ride bikes through town — whatever works for your family. There is an adage that is often used by health and fitness experts: *Move your feet before you eat.*

Schedules are important not only for the school year but also through the summer months. You can have your children brainstorm fun experiences they want to add to their summer schedule like swimming for exercise, identifying insects and animals on hikes, and the zoo. It is still very important to keep reading time as part of everyday as there is always a summer slide.)

5

Developing Good Habits

"Chess is basically a search for truth, right?"

~ Tobey Maguire in *Bobby Fischer*

L ike brushing your teeth twice each day and washing your hands before you eat to reduce bad bacteria, creating daily rituals can give some of the biggest payoffs for better health and well-being. And, since good nutrition is paramount to a successful, long life, it is important to educate children through *every* meal. Balanced meals and appropriately sized portions begin with early childhood and the information is plentiful for young children.

WIC (Woman, Infants, Children) is a non-government agency that helps parents develop good diets for themselves and their families. WIC uses brilliant pictures and descriptions of the portions appropriate to each of the early stages of childhood. Another wealthy source of information is SNAP (Supplemental Nutrition Assistance Programs). Depending on various qualifications, SNAP provides help with food stamps and diet choices for homes with economic restrictions, but that help should also take place at the schools.

Some of the work I was most proud of as a principal was contributing to a better lunch program in our district's public schools. It wasn't easy to fight the system or fix it, but the work was worth the effort.

Our school was the first to sign up for the Second Chance Breakfast Program. Through the program, students received breakfast at morning recess, and not just the beginning of the day before school started (many of our families often came late for multiple reasons). However, even the sugar-filled cereals, or the cellophane wrapped sticky pastry the students obtained during morning recess wasn't really adding to any nutritional solutions for our students.

At one district meeting, filled with over 100 people from all branches of the city, the community was ready to talk about children and nutrition. Most people knew food served in schools often carried little nutritional value. Our school wanted better for the students. Several teachers dared me to bring servings of what the district gave our students *that day* for breakfast and lunch to the meeting.

So, I did.

I carried in the wrapped sticky pastry and a Styrofoam plate filled with nachos and a packet of Kraft cheese (the cheese was still frozen.) I placed it on the table in front of everyone in the large room.

"This" I said, pointing to the food, "is what our school is serving today for the two meals that our student may only get to eat. This is what parents think we are serving as *real* meals. My biggest concern is what are we teaching kids? Are we really saying *this* food is good for you? I'm having a real problem with this. I'm going to bet that our children are going home and *believing* that if they serve this as a meal in school, it must be *good* for you, right?"

Eyes opened, no one in the room said a word. This was one of many instances where I could have easily been reprimanded as a principal. But sometimes, you need to fight for what is right.

After the meeting, one of the school nurses and I were appointed to work with the nutrition department to develop better school meals. And we did our best. For the next two years, we talked about the large amount of sugar and fats in meals and food items with no nutritional value. After a year of discussion and negotiation (everything in the education system is slow to move forward), we signed our school up to be the pilot for the first new lunch program.

Later, as an administrative representative of the school district, we signed up for a Kaiser Grant. The money would be used to take a metric profile of the elementary students' BMI (Body Mass Index) within the district. The study showed that chronic diabetes and heart disease in adults could be charted back as *early onset diabetes* in elementary school.

The High School Nursing Pathway students dressed in their lab uniforms and helped with the height and weight measurements. It was very discreet. We shared the height but not the weight with students, so they wouldn't feel bad or get teased.

The results were frightening.

Close to 40 percent of our district's students (who were in our lowest economic schools) were on track for obesity according to the research. The money from the grant was used to educate our parents in these schools. Interviews with families showed that, several nights a week, parents went to McDonald's for dinner because it was quick and affordable. Also, our parents bought chips of all kinds (cheaply in bulk) as snacks for hungry kids left alone while parents worked.

I mention this because there are easy, affordable meals we can all make that go back to ancient times. Those meals call for simple boiling as a prep but can balance meals nutritiously. I am referring to meal items such as beans, rice, and veggies (perhaps adding chicken or fish as a protein in a meal).

We all know that sugar and fatty foods should not be introduced too early. Children will find it on their own early enough, and it becomes addictive. The carbs change to sugar.

I volunteer in schools around the world. I was very impressed that in Greek elementary school children were required to bring a hot lunch from home and a healthy snack for recess. All students had a stainless-steel container with their surname on it. They went to the kitchen area where an aide put them in an oven under a warm setting. When lunchtime occurred, each of the students went, table by table, to get their lunch and carefully placed a little towel as a tablecloth under their food. Many of their hot lunches were leftovers from the meal the night before.

The meals were so impressive. Chicken and rice, noodles, and vegetables. I found myself envious of their warm, nutritious comfort food. And even if students didn't finish the meal, it was never thrown out. That student brought home what they didn't eat. This cycle helped give the parent feedback about what their child was eating each day.

As parents we need to educate the whole child, which includes good nutrition and daily exercise.

In our American schools, we may provide free and reduced price lunches and breakfasts but do our children even eat it? At my first school, children received their free lunch, took one bite, and then jumped up and threw the rest away to go out and play on the playground. To stop this, I changed the venue setup. The school began playing music. And we made sitting at a table a mandatory twenty minutes. This made the children sit with their food (which made them more likely to eat it) before they could get up and go to the playground.

Studies have also shown that *all screen time* should be limited each day to *no more than two hours*, as suggested by the American Academy of Pediatrics. This includes digital games, smart phones, television, and online learning. The Academy has listed the negative effects, which include negative delays in development and, more importantly, the overall well-being of the child. Over time, children can also acquire inconsistent sleep patterns, *problems with behavior*, and issues keeping their attention.

(In 2023 the Surgeon General called the use of social media by children an "urgent public health issue." It names social media as the main contributor to depression and anxiety, as well as fostering violence and hate in our nation's teenagers—the average teenager is on social media an average of 3.5 hours a day.)

The above information impresses upon all of us that we should actively monitor social media time and content in our children's lives. The Pandemic also gave us time to pause and reevaluate how we structure our world. If we really watch, look, and listen, **children teach us** how they learn best. This was true before Covid-19, and it is true now. We need to tune into what motivates and connects each child to what will best help them develop a purpose-filled happy life.

EXCITE

To create enthusiasm, eagerness, or make ecstatic.

The word "gravity" came up in a lesson. The teacher tried to explain that the rotation of the earth caused a force that pushed objects back down to the earth. But then she changed her learning strategy.

"Okay, I have an idea. Pull out a sheet of paper and watch how I fold the paper." Showing them, she explained, "Fold the top edges into the center line."

She had all the students make a plane and line up to go to the field. You could feel their excitement as students rushed to the line and moved to the field. Once at the field and ready, the teacher called out, "Now, on the count of three, launch your planes as high as you can throw them." The students aimed and fired on three. Quickly, the planes returned to earth, and the students picked them up. Once they had them, they gathered and sat in a circle.

"So, my question is, why didn't they just keep on flying into outer space?" the teacher asked. Then, the lesson began.

6

Turn Everything into a Game

*"Chess is a game that shapes the mind of a person
and played for self-betterment."*

~ BENJAMIN FRANKLIN

"If it isn't fun, I won't come."

I remember a wise teacher quoting this mantra in an Open House meeting with parents. Realistically, we know that learning can sometimes be arduous and challenging, but if you can try to create a game around the important concepts, children will always play to win the right to be first in line. A simple game will increase engagement *every time*. Games increase the answer to every student's internal question:

WHY should I try to remember these facts or analyze an answer?

A third-grade teacher calls groups to line up. Every child wants to be first in line for recess or lunch. "We are going to skip count by threes." The children begin to get excited. She says, "six" then asks, "What's next?" The student who answered nine was chosen to be next in line. The next child says "eighteen", and the teacher says, "Nope. Next." The following child answers "twelve", and she says, "Right!" That student moves into the line (skip counting is another way to reinforce multiplication at an early age).

Children are always motivated and attentive to play a game.

One first-grade teacher has students view the pocket chart outside the door. It is filled with the sight words they learned that morning. Each child picks up a word, hands it to the teacher and tells her the word.

"F-r-o-m," says one child. They spell and say "from", then walk in the door and go to their seat. This simple activity gives teachers a good idea of how many students in her class know the words. If that teacher uses the same ten words, students who may not have known the words will watch and learn them quickly from the others so they can get into the room first.

I watched a first-grade teacher utilize the vocabulary walls she had up for months. Each time the class learned a new vocabulary word, she wrote it on a large card and placed it on the wall. Unfortunately, when the students were doing guided writing lessons, they weren't looking at the wall to find and spell the word correctly.

Children are always motivated and attentive to play a game.

"I have been trying for months for them to learn the words on the wall. I realized just putting them up wasn't working," said the teacher. She shared that, as a new approach, she made the students sit on the carpet and tossed a beanbag to a student and said, "Can you come up and toss the beanbag and hit the word 'yesterday'?"

Everyone watched anxiously as the students searched from one end of the wall to the other. Upon finding the word 'yesterday', the student tossed the beanbag and hit the word with it. The entire class cheered. She then rewarded the student with earning a point for their group. This went to the daily total, which contributed to the chance to clean up first at the end of the day.

The power of being first, or getting to pick first, is always an engaging tool to use with young children. One year, as principal, I turned all the games on the playground into math games. After all, we were a STEM school, and it was STEM celebrations week (a week filled with math and science games). I took the fifth-grade officers of the school's student council out with me to develop game sheets for each area.

In the foursquare courts, we drew a large X through the middle. The direction card told students to count how many squares and triangles they could see. Next, we went to the half dozen numberless hopscotch games stenciled in by workers from the district. We went to each game and wrote in different sets of numbers on each box with a set of instruction cards.

The first had your regular sequence of numbers and the directions explained that the first one to add their numbers and get 20 would win the game. The next hopscotch game had money instead of numbers: 5 cents, 10 cents, and 25 cents. The instruction said that the first one who makes it closest to a dollar wins. There were other hopscotch locations for intermediate students with decimals and fractions. During that week, I felt I could have written an activity book on these forgotten boxes and use them for every school playground I encountered. It was also shocking to me to see how many children had *never played hopscotch.*

As parents and teachers, we have so much curriculum to get through, and we rarely have time to play games. However, it is that spur-of-the-moment game we make out of what we are doing that will capture the attention of a child. We need those games as much as we need the structure and schedules. They all serve to inspire students to learn something for a reason.

7

Creating Young Mathematical Thinkers

"Chess is the art of analysis."

~ Mikhail Botvinnik

Educators put a lot of emphasis on language development because it is the important first step to understanding and communicating in our world. However, math is equally important for interpreting the world around us. It is, after all, the M in STEM.

Math is, and will continue to be, one of the most important transferable skills for future jobs. Working with robotics, AI (artificial intelligence), accounting, interpretation of data, business, systems analytics, coding, engineering and, of course, all the sciences have a fundamental need for solid math skills.

As we learn math, we discover it is a world of symbols and words. But those symbols are not about sounds, they are about **value**. That value can also be represented in different figures and forms children can understand. For instance, the symbol (1) can mean: 1 whole thing, the word *one*, 1 cent, .01, or 1/100. It all represents the same value, whichever term you use. Children need to understand quickly that letters create words in language. And in math, each number or digit has value that can be represented in different ways while still having the same value. If we take toddlers at their "eager-to-learn stage" and show them multiple ways to show the value of numbers, we can learn to create mathematical thinkers early.

One of the easiest visual ways for young children to begin to understand value is to have them count things. Telling a toddler, "Bring me five blocks, hand me five straws," helps them to add experiential learning to a simple request. A simple game for three- and four-year-olds is to take a deck of cards and have the children pull a card. Let's say the number on the card is four. Have the child count four straws or you can show them four pennies (I prefer pennies, and you will see why in Chapter 7 for my rationale for incorporating pennies and real money in teaching value). Each child takes turns and after five turns, the one who has created the highest value wins the round.

You don't need to research the internet to understand how little importance is given to math in American schools. It is a pet peeve of mine. Often it is given so little time in our curriculum and is still so widely dictated by the textbook industry. Conceptually, if a child does not understand that these mathematical sentences called equations represent value, they become lost, and believe they are no good at math. A recent USA Today article written by Erin Richards stated that often "Math Phobia" and "Math Anxiety" begin in elementary school. She believed many elementary teachers didn't understand it themselves and did not give it adequate time and varied ways of learning it.

The textbooks move rapidly forward, losing some students in expanded forms such as 24 is (20) +(4) without having students experience it 'hands-on' with manipulatives.

Is 24 greater than (>)1 or less than (<)1 and what other numbers can add up to be 24? (11) + n = 24. Using manipulatives can help a student get a firmer grasp of numbers. Children need to build these concepts in their head through patterns of reasoning. One can reason that we know 12 plus 12 equals 24. If I know 11 is one less than 12, then the other addend (number that reaches 24) must be 13.

The goal is to maintain interest and make connections in math. When children are ages three and four, have them count, out loud, up and down to 10. After you are certain they have that concept, expand counting to 20. Count by ones, then twos, then fives.

The best tip for developing mathematical understanding is for children to learn how to add and take away in their head (mentally) and then explain their thinking. Start with the concept of addition. One helpful tool for addition is pulling apart numbers. By age five, try having your child begin doubling numbers (1+1=2), (2+2=4), (3+3=6) and so on. This leads to building one of the first mental analytical skills.

A first-grade student should be able to solve 7+8= n in their head, not by memorizing the facts, but by **using the double tool**. A child can explain their answer something like this, "I knew 7+7=14, and 8 is one more than 7, so the answer for n must be 15." Unfortunately, many teachers, like the rest of us, learned mathematics in simple strands and memorization techniques. The problem with memorizing anything is, if you don't use it all the time, you lose it.

Current textbooks are aligned to common core standards and want you to use analytical thinking in word problems that include multiple steps. Children who are not reading at their grade level or can't follow the quick sets of progression set forth by the book's curriculum give up early and believe they will never be good at math. We cannot allow them to believe this is true.

If we take toddlers at their "eager-to-learn stage" and show them multiple ways to show the value of numbers, we can learn to create mathematical thinkers early. For instance, I played with a three-year-old recently and told him to bring me everything that showed me the value of one. I, of course, had lots of representations already on the table. He put down one block, then a die that showed one dot, then one penny, then one straw, then a picture with one cat until he had ten items in a row. I would keep doing this until we reached ten items over multiple times, and then we could start with the mathematical sentences such as 4+3=n.

I found, as an elementary school principal, that language was far more difficult to develop in students — especially second language learners. But mathematics truly could be taught without language. It was my experience that, if a child wanted to look smart in a classroom, they often chose to become more powerful in mathematics.

I discovered that the key to mathematics was the world of counting. As soon as babies start walking, we need to start counting. With each step we count one, two, three... each time they go a little farther we say, "Yes, you did seven steps."

Immediately, there is a value added to the steps. The cheer was to reinforce we went farther. We counted again when we are going up the stairs and down the stairs. By two, your child is chanting along with you as you walk together.

Try playing with racing cars on the floor and have the children take out all their cars. Always have them count their cars first. "Wait a minute," you say. "Last time you counted ten cars. But now, you only have nine cars. How many are missing?" or "Oh, wait a minute, didn't you have four red cars? Now you only have three. Where is the other one?"

There are quite a few tricks children can learn by utilizing mathematical thinking. Most of it is transferring value. Here is an opportunity to help your child with that very concept:

Create a number line somewhere in the house. One family placed a 10-foot line of masking tape down the center of their main hallway with numbers marked on them from 0 at the start to 30 at the finish. This was a good choice because the American standard for entering kindergarten is that children need to be able to count numbers from 1 to 30.

They also need to be able to count to 100, by ones, twos, fives, and tens by the time they finish kindergarten.

It really isn't that hard if it becomes part of their everyday play. So, the toddlers armed with their race cars would have a race to see which of their four cars went farthest down the hall. By the age of three, they could see the number 12 and circle it on the chart on the wall. By four, they could write the biggest number on a whiteboard. After their race, the three toddlers had a comparison of numbers.

Ask, "So, which one went the farthest?" They know that the biggest number wins, but what is the biggest number? By using the number line on the floor, all of them can see that the car that went to 12 traveled the farthest. The car that went to 8 didn't go as far.

Comparison and association of value needs to be communicated as often as possible. By age five, students can create tally strokes and learn the trick that after every four strokes, they can make a diagonal slash through the four and now they can count bigger numbers by fives to see who won the most races.

In most households there is a variation of ages. Younger children can't conceptualize as quickly as their older siblings. But the older children can be helpers, and this too can be made into an earning opportunity. Older children can get the job of writing the numbers and calling out the totals to help their younger siblings understand the value associated with the numbers.

Take every opportunity to translate number values. Every time blocks or Legos come out of the bin, it is important to ask how many pieces you have when they start. Have toddlers line them up and count them. If they mix numbers up, have them go to the nearby number chart and see what number they missed. Number lines and charts that display 1-100 can be used for many games.

Once children are in kindergarten, they can be asked to put their finger on a double-digit number like 12. You can also ask if the number is odd or even. Of course, 12 is even, but when the child puts their finger on 33, it would be odd. If you have three children in the house, you might think of buying three small hundred charts or making them on a sheet of paper to use as a tool.

Each child can pick a number. Let's say one picks 6. Then move your piece up 10 more. They move their piece to 16. Now say move it back by 2, and they know the number they should look for is 14.

Last week, I visited a school playground. The school had the usual vacant hopscotch boards, a United States Map with no words, a compass with degree marks, and a very large circle called a clock that had 60 segment lines with longer interval lines for every five minutes. It had no numbers and no hands. I thought it was brilliant. I quickly took my tribe of five- and seven-year-olds over to the circle.

"So, what is this?" I asked.

None of them guessed it was a clock. Of course, the circle had no numbers. However, it had a symbol that showed the bezel.

"Okay, for fifty cents, how many little lines are marked inside the circle?"

The five-year-olds began counting the lines as the seven-year-olds watched and realized that the longer segments counted by fives. He quickly had the answer, but I told him to whisper the number in my ear.

When everyone finished whispering 60, I asked them, "60 what?" The seven-year-old said, "Minutes." Then I asked, "How many seconds in a minute?" He didn't know the answer, so he Googled it.

"60," he answered.

Any time you can have young learners get up and jump or run around while counting the minutes and seconds, that experience becomes more than play for them. But if they didn't see how it works on a playground, using pencil and paper can still help them. Either way, they are getting it because it is reinforced as a game.

In the schools where I worked, one of the most valuable thirty minutes in a teacher's day was called the "Math Wall." The wall was set up with examples of a dozen different strands and covered in that year's common core. Over the year, the examples and numbers would get more complicated. However, the repetition of the different strands daily over the course of the year gave students a brilliant overview of what they needed to know and a progressive way to teach math concepts. Students who struggled were given smaller numbers and easier equations. Higher level students were given more challenging equations using more complicated numbers such as fractions and decimals.

Third grade students would take the daily temperature in Fahrenheit and Celsius, and by third grade they might be graphing the times on a chart for sunrise to sunset for each day. It was amazing to watch the graph as the days went from longer to shorter each day as fall headed into winter, and then by spring, the days lengthened again. Graphs are perfect visual tools for creating mathematical understanding and creating conversation around math.

In kindergarten, students in public school begin counting how many days they have been in school. They usually celebrate the 100th day of school by bringing in 100 objects from home to show others. There are many item choices, such as beans or stickers, so they can conceptualize the amount. Teachers will often have an adult dress up as "Zero the Hero." The costume itself has two large zeros on the front. "We are now into three-digit numbers," says the teacher. "The more zeros at the end, the bigger the number. See, this one after you add four zeros is a thousand. A thousand is a four-digit number. Ten thousand is a five-digit number."

I must admit I'm still appalled that we allow children to count on their fingers in classes after first grade (discounting special needs.). Counting on fingers is a crutch, not a tool. Would you give a child a crutch to learn to walk? Maybe this was needed initially, but you know you have to take it away eventually, or they will always need a crutch and will believe they will not be able to walk without one. I still visit fourth and fifth grade classrooms and there are still students counting on fingers. If children haven't been given ample time to solve simple addition and subtraction in their heads, they might always need this crutch.

If I'm teaching in an intermediate classroom, I usually play a quick card game of '99' at the end of each day. You play the game with a regular deck of cards (you can find the rules to this quick, easy game online with a simple Google search). The trick is to have children count in their heads what the overall value is on the table when they add a card. It gives the perfect mental opportunity for counting up. Like learning to tie their own shoes, children are pressured into mentally counting with games of this nature, mainly because they fear being embarrassed in front of their peers for not knowing.

Even students with learning delays can learn to build the tool of doubles and go up and down to find answers in their head. By using single digit numbers in number sentences such as: 6+3=n, they can stack, and then backtrack. A child answers, "3 plus 3 equals 6. I knew this answer first because I know my doubles, and I know the number 6 was 3 more, so I added it to my answer of 6 and decided 9 was my final answer."

One fourth grade teacher shared a strategy she came up with to overcome the fear of memorizing multiplication facts. Like anything we memorize, the facts disappear from our brains if we do not use them all the time.

"I told my students that if they knew the 6 through 9 times tables, they knew *all* of the tables," she said. "But even just saying that proved to be too difficult for some of my students."

"So, I came up with this idea to develop a tool box before each math lesson. The students needed to create an array (a grid of 1 to 12 across the top horizontal line, and 6 to 9 down the left vertical line.) I instructed them to fill in the grid using skip counting. (6 and 6 more is 12 and so on until they filled in the entire line. Then they proceeded to sevens, eights, and nines. After a week, I set a timer when they finished, and they wrote their time below the grid. I gave the students a ticket for our weekly lottery if they beat the time from the day before. They were competing with themselves."

The teacher reported it was like magic. Within a month, every student could fill in the array in less than five minutes. The students' confidence levels rose exponentially, and they learned to use the tool to check their work. Soon her students' scores went up, as did those of her PLC team (professional learning community). It didn't take long for the school to embrace the effect of students developing their own tool bars as practice each day. Fifth grade students drew a simple number line with a zero in the middle placing the numbers one through four to the right and left from zero and dividing them into quarters. This handy tool helped students visualize fractions and decimals more easily.

The future is about science and data. Math knowledge is an important skill for the future.

There are many books written around creating mathematical understanding. One author of note is the guru Marilyn Burns. In a school with many English learners, the mathematical software created by Dr. Matthew Peterson on ST Math (Spatial Temporal Math) created a way to lead students through all sequences of math without the use of language. Set up like a computer game, the small penguin Jiji will move completely across the screen if the student solves the problem. (A product of Mind Institute).

One of my schools' Site Council visited an Orange County school that had almost perfect math scores. Students at Weaver Elementary played 20-minute sequenced ST Math games when they finished other work each day. Its ability was to fill in gaps with sequence of patterns using no language. The students kept track of their progress each day. The systems would supply more experiences if a student was unable to solve the problem. To children, this support was a game they would seek out at the end of each day. Mind Institute became so involved with the project that it helped develop music piano keyboard lessons that assisted fourth and fifth grade students translate the language of music into fractions.

Weaver Elementary had it all going on. They had Math Walls, CGI (Cognitive Guided Instruction) math problems, ST Math, and music. Math was taught at least two hours a day. When my students' parents visited the school, they wanted it for our students and the PTO began yearly fundraising campaigns to phase in this focus of support. It impacted our scores in a positive way.

Erin Richards also featured another California school in her article "Math Scores Stink in America." In this USA Today article in 2020, she applauded a Sweetwater High School 12th grade math class entitled "Discreet Math" which was developed in partnership with San Diego State University. They explored topics like two-player games, graph theory, sequence theories and cryptography. They even played a Capture the Flag game that emphasized mathematics. The teacher is always being asked by students, "Is this really math?"

Recent reports place California students at only 30% proficient in mathematics by the eighth grade. I believe we can do so much better than that if we apply math wherever we can.

A month ago a grandfather shared with me that he was helping his grandson with his sixth-grade math.

"Are you getting him to *apply* the math or are you just going through the problems in the book," I asked.

"What do you mean?" he said.

"You're working on proportions, right?" He nodded, staring incredulously, and wondering how I knew that.

"Well, here is an idea. Tell him you are throwing a party for a dozen people. Look up the recipes that are only for four and see if he can increase each recipe to accommodate for twelve. Come on, it will be fun."

He agreed and smiled, offering a "Thanks."

8

Earning Power

"The pin, in chess, is mightier than the sword."
(A pin is a tactic you can use to restrict one or
more of your opponent's pieces.)

~ FRED REINFELD

It is only now that educators are speaking out about the importance of connecting one's education with real life, but many of us already knew it always had the greatest impact. Young children are curious to learn more about the real world so, as educators, we should be helping to build those bridges. Any time they can roleplay an adult role, a child fulfills their quest to see how they can fit their own interest and passion within that world.

Earning power is an overarching theme of the work world. It is an energy that not only feeds the overall theme of life, but also rewards one's effort. As a parent, guardian, grandparent, or teacher, you may not be on board at first with the idea of rewarding effort with real money.

I understand your argument. *Why should I reward one's motivation when it should come internally?*

There is a lot of research around "intrinsic" motivation (that "internal reward"). Not many people seem to have it in the American adult workforce. However, "extrinsic" motivation (giving someone a tangible reward or a reason to do something) is often needed to give the impetus for becoming motivated. There are even studies supporting the idea that getting paid at a job is part of a person's intrinsic motivation to work.

Anything that hits a pleasure zone motivates people (the Pavlov theory). Video games hit the zone by creating a game (which we already know is pleasurable to children).

Children, like most adults, can become intrinsically motivated by things they want to learn more about. However, in areas surrounding the basic Three R's (reading, writing, and 'rithmetic), many children find obstacles and just want to quit or give up. One of the most important skills that needs to develop early in childhood is "grit."

Consider what happened when I purchased a new bedroom set for my son which included a tall bureau. I had a neighbor help me with a bedframe, but later I mused at the directions for putting together the bureau with complete despair. After sorting through dozens of different sized screws and different sized boards, I threw my hands up in front of my eight-year-old son and said, "I can't do this. I should have paid the extra twenty dollars and had the shop send a laborer out to put this together."

It was summer vacation, but as a principal I needed to go to work the next day.

My youngest son looked at the small print and pictures of the diagram and said, "Will you pay me the twenty dollars to put it together?"

I looked at the directions and back at him, he was a struggling reader how could he possibly tackle this?

"It's all yours. You want to try it, the money is yours."

The next morning I found him carefully examining all the pieces on the rug in his room.

"Listen I'll be home at 3. Don't worry if you can't do it. I'll call the shop to bring someone out tomorrow. You just won't have a bureau for a night or two."

Later that day I walked in the front door to see my son beaming. "Come see."

Standing erect as the Eiffel Tower on the far wall stood a tall perfectly finished walnut bureau. There were no pieces of anything on the floor.

"Did you do this yourself?" I asked in disbelief.

"Yes."

"How?"

"I did it step-by-step following the picture directions." He answered proudly.

"You're hired!" I said as I ran for my purse. I took out thirty dollars and handed it to him.

"That's the best and most efficient job I have ever seen anyone do. From now on, I will always offer you the job first."

Grit comprises a few vital character traits such as: resilience, persistence, and confidence. Think about a child who is playing the game *Minecraft*. They will continue to demonstrate the grit it takes to bring the player to the next level. The game incorporates why, and the players continue to pursue learning the game because of this.

However, when reading gets too hard or math feels like it is too complicated, children will most often just give up. We can't allow our children to just give up because, as life-long learners, there will always be *more* to learn. Grit is a very needed skill for our future learners.

As parents, we often need to promote the incentive as to *why* they need to learn something that is challenging. I watched a father handle the situation to help develop his sons' grit, persistence, and resilience. His six-year-old son kept shouting for his dad to help him figure out how to put a Lego kit together. The dad had all three of his children needing his attention at the same time — the eighteen-month-old and a three-year-old toddler were screaming the loudest.

"Dad, I need help putting this Lego kit together!" yelled the six-year-old from the other room.

"Oh, you can figure that out. First look at the pictures on the box."

"I did dad. I can't figure it out."

"I think maybe you can. Just take a moment and pull the paper out with the instructions. I'll be there in just a minute."

The wise dad stayed away a good thirty minutes and returned later to see how his son was doing. *Never come to the rescue right away, push the pause button.* This can cause the child to take initiative and problem-solve.

"How did you make out?" asked the dad entering the child's bedroom.

"I did it! I figured it out! I just went down one step at a time." The little boy was motivated to figure it out knowing his dad was too busy to help. The dad never said he was too busy. He just continued to encourage his son to take his time and persevere.

We need to continue to encourage children so they can build the grit needed to get through each task. With each successful project, your child builds confidence, which is the gift that keeps on giving.

As a means of "growing grit" through earning power, many teachers reward children with stickers in classrooms. After earning a certain number of stickers, (token economy system) children may earn a privilege.

We should incentivize the question, "WHY should I learn this?" As a school principal, I began working with business and software experts who were creating novel, intricate ways to design allowances for students of a certain age. Their goal was to promote allowances with the purpose of helping students grow and plan an economic future. I began to think, why are we asking them to wait to a certain age to understand money when real money transfers into mathematical thinking? There are studies to support the theory for children to begin earning allowances at age five. Most old-school thinkers believed that earning an allowance could only develop business sense, but I believe it can accomplish so much more.

I recently consulted with some young parents who were trying to construct not only learning environments, but also to locate appropriate homeschool activities and games to help their children learn beyond the distance learning mode. It was becoming evident some parents wanted to fill the gap. Even though their children did not learn the same, they were all eager to learn a new game to play. I had the preschool-aged children sit and trace letters on a whiteboard. After eight minutes, they were done with trying, so I asked, "Who wants to play a game?"

They all replied by eagerly raising their hands.

I went over to the alphabet rug in the middle of their bedroom. It was time to move to a physical game. I told them, "Okay, we are going to take turns." I looked at one boy, and said, "We are going to start with you." I tossed him the beanbag. "Run over and drop it on the letter "W" and then come back to the board and write the letter "W" on the board. When you're finished, you get a penny." The children beamed.

"A real penny?" they asked.

"Yes. When you play with me, you always get real money to put in your bank."

I keep the banks happy by running in each week and exchanging my dollars for coins. My motivation for using money (coins) is to build number sense by creating a real worth that can be used later to transfer to larger numbers of earning. This can grow into compound concepts like spending and saving.

I gave each of the students a little zipper bank bag with their name on it (I bought those at Staples). Before they counted their pennies to put in the bag, I asked if anyone had five pennies they wanted to trade for a nickel. All of them did, so we traded some of their pennies for nickels.

I told them their banking day would be Friday, and they could trade more of the coins in for bigger coins then. By Friday, each child had at least five nickels to trade for a quarter and by the next week they traded four quarters for a dollar bill. In their mind they were getting rich. In the beginning they thought the heavier the bag got, the richer they were.

They also began to notice that changing a hundred pennies for a dollar bill made the bag lighter, but they now understood the concept that they still had the same amount/value in the bag.

Most preschool students do not understand value yet. So, I asked the homeschooling parents if they might be up for creating a store at their snack time. We decided to make the experience even more real by assigning a child shopkeeper for the day to stand behind a counter.

The parents created a shop that had four possible snacks the children could spend their hard-earned money on. A cracker with peanut butter cost one cent, apple slices cost two cents, a yogurt container went for five cents, and a licorice stick for two cents. We were playing store, but they were really shopping. The children shopped and we *all* realized the power given to the children with the opportunity to play and imagine a real setting.

Grit is the fiber of the learner. It helps build the resilience and persistence needed for being a life-long learner.

It would be a while before the children would be able to count the change back, but we created a real-life learning opportunity. Staging events like this will help children understand that earning power becomes spending power.

I can't tell you how much confidence comes from playing learning games with real money. Immediately, there are so many built-in options for lifelong education. For one, the number sense is immediately enhanced. Every day I was there, the children were getting opportunities around value. I suggested to the mother, "When you walk in a store and the kids want something, you can now just turn to them and ask if they have enough money in their bank bag to buy it." Let's change the screaming of "I want that," to "Can I afford that?"

Children pick up quickly that they can earn the power to get something they want. Parents always have a power struggle with children; it is an everyday occurrence. We often pick and choose our battles. Sometimes we cave on issues where we really shouldn't have, like letting them eat another cookie before dinner, or letting them go outside before they finished their work because they were screaming for you to let them go.

Don't feel bad; we have all done it.

But every time we let it happen, they have learned that screaming and crying gets them what they want. So, what if there was another way to handle this?

What if you used earning power as a teaching tool and as a reward system for good behavior? By the time a child turns five, you can establish a system with benefits and fines. A chart is usually in a very visible place such as the refrigerator or a bulletin board listing chores like making the bed, picking up the toys, putting your dirty dishes in the dishwasher or clothes in a hamper. If they do these chores without being told, they can earn some money at the end of their week, or you can change it to immediate rewards like quarters each time they finish a chore.

Fines are usually around the cultured behavior set in schools and homes.

Schools usually post some version of the Three Bs — **Be** respectful, **Be** responsible, and **Be** safe (and **Be Kind**). Your house may have rewards for kindness and respect and a fine for fighting and tantrums. Nothing is more upsetting to a child than having to get their bank bag and shell out money for fines, but each lesson helps to build character in children.

Society is full of rules. If you are speeding on the highway and the police pull you over, he or she may hand you a ticket with a fine. If you are parked in a spot and you didn't put money in the meter, you might get a fine. So, everyone learns quickly they don't want to get a fine.

The list of rewards and fines of course can be changed as parents find that certain behaviors need to change. An infraction doesn't necessarily need to be listed on the chart either.

Any time a child does something that could earn them a "Time out", you could also add a fine. Not listening, back talking, running out into the street, hitting or biting anyone, telling a lie, taking something from a store shelf, all go under the Three Bs. Those mistakes in judgment can cost them real money.

Some behaviors deserve a substantial fine to get a child's attention. No child wants to deplete their savings if it takes away from their goal of buying something they want. Remember, as a parent, you are not there to be the *friend* but the *parent*. Everything that you allow to occur when a rule is broken gives the child the unspoken permission to do it again. If you have more than one child, they all learn (at that same moment of infraction) that it was okay to break that rule.

Sometimes as parents we become our own enemy when we do this. The consequence is having to rebuild the rules and the consistency all over again.

We can minimize the number of times we need to address any issue by simply getting a child's attention. If your child has been saving up for something they really wanted to have, and we take some of what they earned as a fine, it usually is enough of an impact for them not to do it again. When a child begins saving up for something over time, they begin to recognize the significance of goals.

EXPLORE

To inspect, transverse, delve, probe, or go deeper.

"Halloween is a week away, so my question is,
are all pumpkins the same?" asked the teacher.
Almost in unison the class called out,
"They are all different!"
"All of them?"
"Yes."
"Okay. Over the next week I want you to tell me in how many
ways they are all different." "Bring in your pumpkin
so we will measure, weigh, draw, see if they float, and cut
into each and see if they are different inside."

9

Short- and Long-term Goals

"In chess, strategy requires thought, tactics require observation."

~ Max Euwe

By the time a child is six or seven, they have a desire to buy bigger things. Now we can introduce the idea of saving money and not spending it in stores for immediate rewards. We can also introduce waiting and saving up for something bigger (such as a video game they want to buy).

It becomes increasingly more powerful when children ask you what other chores they can do to pick up some more cash. Times like this are great for parents to introduce the concept of shopping.

A parent might say, "You know, I noticed that Walmart always has a sale on that game during the holidays."

Now you have the child's full attention.

Your child not only knows where to buy the game, but they can also use less of their money. It is amazing how fast behaviors come in line with earning power.

Children avoid fines at all costs and want to do more to earn more money. They may begin bargaining with you for rewards if they finish projects early or earn high grades for school projects. When this happens, parents have a great bargaining tool. Look at the increased motivation. Why? Because people need a reason to care, to do just about anything.

So, make games around shopping. When you begin shopping in stores, you can play a game with your young school-age children, such as the following:

"I need to find the beans that are the cheapest — a nickel for who can find it first."

Or "How much is that loaf of bread, or that jar of peanut butter?"

Or perhaps you can suggest, "When you get to the counter, there is a quarter to the one who can get closest to the amount of money the bill comes to, and another for how much money I need to pull out of my wallet to give to the clerk."

This is called *shopping engagement.*

I know, as parents, most often we pay with debit or credit cards when we shop. But by pulling out twenty-dollar bills, you can give children the concept that all this costs *real* money and you need to pull out at least five twenty-dollar bills to pay for these groceries.

Another bonus could result when a parent asks, "Can you tell me how much change the clerk will give me if I give him five twenty-dollar bills?"

By the time your child turns 10 (perhaps before), this weekly system of exchange of money has transferred mathematical knowledge into fractions and decimals. It isn't a mystery to them that one cent is 1/100 of a dollar, that a nickel is 5/100 of a dollar and that it takes twenty of them to make a dollar. Skilled with these tools, they can transfer the value to everything else mathematically.

And this, too, can be rewarded.

Whatever day you designate to be Banking Day is a perfect time to praise children for making their goal. By the time a child has reached

$50 in their bank bag, I encourage parents to open a bank account and have a sponsored bank card that is linked to your account. That way, you can check how the money is being spent. With young children, this isn't a big problem, however, with older children it can be. You definitely want to supervise what they are buying and who they are buying it from. My suggestion would be for parents to keep the bank card and guide conversation about its usage. Many banks offer special accounts for kids that are linked to a parent's bank account. Having a bank card is another link to the real world which empowers a child to think they are already a productive consumer.

As children get older (around age nine or ten), it is time to build the concept of saving money. Saving power has *more power* than spending power.

A conversation could begin with, "Do you really think you need to have that new bike right now? It's a couple of hundred dollars. Christmas is in two months. Maybe you can ask for a new one then."

Holding back money to save and grow for the future is always a good idea. You can also introduce the concept of living on a budget. Banking institutions always advise adults to save a minimum of 10% of their income for their future in a 401k plan.

Baiting children with saving for higher level purchases in the foreseeable future works well for them. When my two sons were in middle school, I tempted them with an offer they couldn't refuse. I told them that all young men want to have their own truck/car and their own independence by the time they are 17 years old.

"I'm going to make you a deal. Instead of you buying more video games with your money, what if I help you purchase a vehicle for when you turn 17? I will match whatever you save up before your first job. You'll need several thousand dollars."

Soon after this conversation, I brought home a copy of Auto Trader. I told them to pick out a vehicle they might like. Both boys picked out

Toyota truck models. Then we matched the price in Auto Trader and Kelly Blue Book. My sons each cut out a picture of the truck they wanted to purchase, and we created a vision board in their rooms. They realized the older the vehicle, the lower the cost. Vehicles that were five years old were going for $4500. But I also warned them that the older the vehicle, the more the vehicle might need to be fixed.

"So," I told them, "If you save up all your Christmas and birthday money plus your allowances and, let's say, you save $2000 over the next five years, I will match it and you will have $4000. You will of course need to get a job to pay for gas and insurance when you buy the truck. But, believe me, this is going to be the number one thing you want at age 17."

I put the deal in writing and at that moment they saw themselves as proud "future owners" of trucks. *Now I needed to start a savings account for both boys*, I thought.

I had two reasons for wanting the boys to save up for a vehicle. Besides the power of saving, I noticed that many teens were wrecking the vehicles that were *just* given to them. I felt that, if my sons understood how long it took to save up to purchase a truck, they would take better care of it. There is nothing more memorable than the purchase of your first vehicle.

One couple I worked with shared that their son, Henry, who had decent savings, took a three-month business course in his ninth-grade class. After the course, Henry decided he wanted to invest some of his money to make more money. He talked with his parents, who suggested he take only a small part of his money out of his savings and invest it (they pointed out that there is always a certain risk with investments).

Henry's parents helped him buy some stock in a well-known technology company. He watched the stock go up and down over the year but decided he would just leave the money in, based on his parents' advice. He then took the other half of his investment capital and decided to sell some of the harvested fruits and vegetables from his garden.

He was making some steady (and sustainable) income every week from his little garden stand. Henry was excited, but then he became industrious. He noticed that if he sold other things like baskets and old signs he found in garage sales, and if he refurbished some old furniture and sold it, he could make a steady profit.

Henry had turned into an entrepreneur; he was learning the fundamentals of basic economy. His confidence grew with each sale and his parents continued to guide him to risk only as much as he was willing to lose.

By ten years of age, have children create a vision board of what they would like to save for now and plan for in the future.

With the digital world at each student's fingertips, it is easy for people to pursue e-commerce opportunities to buy and sell goods online. Many adults discovered this concept on eBay and Craigslist. There are many opportunities for students to form companies, establish platforms, and create brands for advertising and selling goods and services.

Statistics tell us that about 65 percent of our "Generation Z" children will have formed an e-commerce company sometime in their life, whether as a part-time job to support their income, or to manufacture or provide services for a full-time business. It makes perfect sense since everyone has access to the internet. Creating early positive experiences is key.

Different children are motivated in different ways. As mentioned in the beginning of this chapter, if you make learning fun like turning it into a game, a simple penny is enough of a reason to get a child's full attention. It answers the "why" should I learn or want to play question. The learning opportunity is the win-win.

EMPOWER

To enable, invest, accredit, authorize, certify, warrant, or give individual ownership.

"This organic garden is going to help supply the cafeteria's salad bar," said the teacher.

"Each of you will form a group of four and develop a plot using compost and heirloom seeds to grow crops for salads. The school will pay us a dollar for every two pounds of produce. You research and decide what is the best crop, organic material, number of seeds, water to add, and harvest time. Let's see which group produces the most and makes the most profit."

10

Middle School, The Land of Missed Opportunities

"A bad plan in chess is better than no plan at all."

~ Frank Marshall

I am of the firm belief that, before their children leave elementary school, parents should begin having conversations with them about the work world. Guided conversations about what their children want to do when they grow up or what **industry** they want to pursue should become an *exploratory theme.* I also need to warn you — it is often the same time children pull away from talking with their parents. This is the time they begin grabbing all their perspective ideas about the world from their peers.

Lots and lots of misinformation comes this way.

Middle school is a stressful time for most parents. Students can't wait for the passage into middle school to share the world of tweens to teens with hundreds of others experiencing their own hormonal imbalances.

I was the mother of two boys, and I wanted them to find their own paths. I'm sure you do, too. Have faith. They always do, but there might be a lot of tears and fears in between now and then. Until the time they turn thirty, people are often exploring their options. Don't be surprised when your child wants to start at the top without putting in the effort to get there. Remember, you were the one who reinforced that they should pursue their dreams.

Unless your child is in a K-8 school or a K-12 school, most students from many different elementary schools have traditionally been sent to one central middle school in Public School Districts. Class sizes go up, new friends are made, and there is a pecking order of students who cluster into groups sharing their same kind of interest, causing acceptance or unacceptance in these tenuous years.

Most private schools keep the classes small through the eighth grade, however public middle schools can be significantly larger. Imagine a group of thirty-eight students in a 900-square-foot classroom. I always want to give our middle school teachers a special hug because they are a special breed.

Currently, most middle schools do not give credits toward college or build experiences toward certifications like high schools do. Many students do not connect to the meaning of *why* they are there except to discover their teenage world of likes and dislikes among peers. Puberty is prevalent and students want to be accepted. The emergence of peer pressure might also be cause for concern. Throughout middle school, students' first images of themselves are reflected by the students they merge with.

But on the journey of life, we must make sure we get the students' attention. Middle school is a perfect time to develop the young adult mind into the work world. Most electives at this level could give students opportunities to explore experiences like robotics, perhaps some digital marketing and sometimes, if a teacher is adventurous, building a business.

We often miss the opportunity to introduce many of the skills that we can nurture throughout our lifetimes, such as: working with wood, connecting pipes, cooking a balanced meal, understanding electrical connections, horticulture, designing clothing, shaping surf boards, cutting hair, repurposing furniture, welding, and the like — in other words, fueling the need to know how things work from someone who knows how to do it. Offering students experiences in *life skills* like these can open their minds and give them lessons and options that can be used again and again throughout their lifetimes.

Recently, I was talking to a Swedish sailor who described all the skills he needed to use on boats while sailing the world. Most of those skills were ones he learned in middle school in Sweden.

"Everyone took woodwork, mechanics, cooking, and sewing," he said. "Just learning the essentials about how things work prepares you to be confident enough to try to fix things yourself before you call in the professional who will charge you at least $80 or more an hour. I not only repair and sew my own sails and canvas but I have sutured people's wounds at sea."

He also shared that in Swedish middle schools each student needed to spend two weeks each summer in an apprenticeship that they set up themselves within an industry.

"My first summer I was certain I wanted to be a vet," he said. " I signed up for my two weeks and quickly decided by the second week it wasn't for me. It was heart breaking to see animals suffering and then be put to sleep. Nope, not for me. But how would I have realized that if I hadn't experienced that work environment?"

Currently, some summer career camps are developing to give students the opportunities to explore the use of different skills. On the first day of the camp, students learn to define who they are and what do they like to spend their time doing (besides playing video games).

What interest could fill their souls with passion and purpose!

Often students entering middle school get online and take a quick **RIASEC** (Realistic, Investigative, Artistic, Social, Enterprising, and Conventional) interest quiz. This 1950s quiz developed by John Holland using psychometric codes is designed to match each individual personality with their interest. In less than thirty minutes, this quiz reveals a list of possible careers you may have an interest in pursuing. (The U.S. Department of Labor maintains a database of occupations sorted using Holland's Code.)

After finishing the RIASEC quiz, the students discuss the differences between a career and a job. I often ask students to interview at least three adults during their first week. One of the questions should be, "Do you remember your first job?"

Everyone begins somewhere. I have often shared my own story with students. I was sixteen, entering my junior year in high school, when I got my working papers from the guidance counselor. That summer, I worked in a local restaurant on the boardwalk down the Jersey Shore. I loved the job so much that I went back every summer during my college years to save money for the next school year.

On the second day of our Career Camp, students create a vision board of where they see themselves in ten years, where and how they are living (are they in a house, are they in the same town, do they own a car?). It is interesting to hear what students see themselves doing for work to be independent, self-sustaining adults.

The following day, students mapped a vision for where they would be in five years and how they are going to get to that ten-year career vision. Students do their homework on what it costs to create and maintain the life they created on their vision board. The next assignment for students is to go home and interview their parents about what it costs to live and maintain a house or a condo in the town where they currently live.

This assignment is usually eye-opening for the parents as well as the students. Armed with a page of questions, the student interviews the parents about how much money it would take to sustain a monthly budget in their current lifestyle. Some parents shared that, through this exercise, they realized part of their financial struggle had been because they were living above their budget.

How much is the monthly rent or mortgage, car payment, gas, internet cost, cost of food, entertainment, movie channels, just going out to dinner once a week or taking in a movie at a cinema? Does this budget include a one-week or two-week vacation for the family to get away once a year?

The last group of students I worked with found that an average small family in their hometown would need close to $85,000 a year to sustain a middle-class lifestyle (cars, house, utilities, food, vacation in 2022). Most students shared that both parents were working and, with their current salaries, could maintain the budget. We then returned to each student's vision board and explored a budget someone would need to maintain a life in the place where they saw themselves in the future. The digital world gives students access to viewing many new and upcoming jobs to enhance such activities.

Career week finishes with students creating a pretend resume that they would send to apply for the job they wish to have within their chosen industry. In the resume, they talk about their certification, where they went to school, and for how long. It also includes work experience each student had over the years, which would prove to the employer they had the essential skills to prepare them to be a good candidate for the position.

At the end of a career course, students shared that it was the *first* time they *ever* thought about what things cost and that they understood much better about steering a course that could provide a better lifestyle for them.

Perspective often comes from fears and doubts we place in our heads. Hearing other perspectives often clears the fog away. In a Socratic Seminar, students go to the area of the room that aligns with the position they share for their answer. Each student speaks about why they support that view. It is a very insightful process. Each child is often prepared to support their point of view but is often intrigued by the positions shared by the other classmates. At one point, there was a Socratic Seminar helping the students answer deeper questions like, do I think I will get close to my vision, or do I think I probably will do something else? I have always found Socratic Seminars beneficial across all subjects.

There are always about a third of the students who truly know what they want to do and are confident that nothing will get in the way of their vision and determination. However, the remaining two-thirds (or more) of the students aren't sure, and really don't know what they want to do or how they hope to get there. I assure those students that, since the beginning of time, most people have felt this way. This is why so many boys used to learn trades from their fathers. If a young boy knew for sure he wanted to do something other than the trade of his father by the age of twelve, he would go live with the person he wanted to apprentice under for the next seven years.

If we head into the future knowing more about ourselves and what makes us happy, we are apt to uncover and go after jobs that fill that need. My advice is always to seize every experience and opportunity to bring children closer to their vision.

Middle school is also the perfect time to interview people who they think have interesting jobs and ask them how they got there. In many cases, it wasn't a straight line but rather a random set of opportunities that led them to their current job.

Each Spring, one of my elementary schools had a Career Day. It was not like the one referenced above. Instead, the school brought in the community to share their careers with people. Women firefighters, marines, local veterinarians, and male nurses graced our halls for a day. We always served them a beautiful lunch often provided as a potluck by the teaching staff. Kick-starting a day set aside to bring in the community is a great start, but having people visit classrooms with their career stories each month is even better.

I ran into a student from one of my schools five years ago. He was all smiles but was worried about his future. He was twenty years old with no job, a pregnant wife, and his mother to care for as well. He needed a job right away that could help him build a future.

Just that week, I met with the new recruiting officer for a new FedEx plant that was opening in the community.

"Listen, you are a great guy and a hard worker. Convince them you will do whatever it takes to work hard for them," I told the former student. "FedEx is a growing industry that builds in opportunities for advancement in many different areas, not to mention provides health care and retirement plans that will help support you through life."

He thanked me, and I later found out that, within a short time, he had taken my advice and had already advanced himself up to the Delivery Management Department at FedEx! Twenty years ago, my sister's boyfriend took up auto mechanics in high school. My sister was in a car accident and the man who hit her gave her his card and said, "I think I can get your boyfriend a job working as an aircraft mechanic for FedEx." The world is huge. And the world is small. It's the stories people share that allow young people to keep their eyes open for opportunities when they present themselves. Young people have been brought up to think big and "live their dreams." But sometimes our feet need to be on the ground running toward the opportunities around us. Conversations with parents need to include that **nothing comes without hard work.** A great way to show this important lesson is shadowing.

Shadowing experiences (following an adult for a day at their job) are truly important during the middle school years. It gives young adults an opportunity to see and feel the environment around what interest they have for a day or week. If a student takes a real interest in the work, they may be able to apprentice the next year (work for a week or two at the job).

If there are no local career camps or skill camps, there could be an opportunity for parents to talk about the nearby work world and what jobs their children can experience in their town. All families have a network of friends and family who work in different trades and careers. School teachers, dentists, cooks, framers, farmers, landscapers, house cleaners, police officers, shopkeepers, mechanics, officer managers and the like would be happy to host your child for a day to shadow them in their job.

It is important for a student to keep a notebook about their experience and log things they liked and things they didn't. Have your child interview the person they are shadowing and include what a person doing their job would earn per hour, week, and month to determine if the job is what they are looking for. Asking those questions clearly shows whether or not that particular job aligns with their future vision.

In my discussions with students, I often share that my oldest son and I missed opportunities to have these conversations. He was an AP student on the honor roll in high school and we talked about college. But what he secretly wanted was a career where he used his hands, figured out problems, and did hard labor (he loved to work out daily at the gym). After four years, many dollars, and a UC bachelor's degree, he graduated with no license to work and began to examine the work world through the lens of what he *really* wanted to learn and do. He began exploring the internet for good paying labor jobs and decided he wanted to be a plumber. He needed to begin an apprenticeship (these jobs paid very little, gave no sick days, and no benefits). My son was getting married but still wanted to live in Santa Barbara where rent is steep! He realized he needed to go back to school to learn a skill that would take years to develop. It was going to be an extra burden he didn't predict in a time with a growing responsibility. After returning to community college for technical training, he earned two more associate degrees required for appropriate licenses dealing with plumbing.

I wonder what advice he is going to give his children when they are in middle school?

I have long imagined Tiny House Projects being introduced at the middle school level. Students in the seventh-grade year may submit a design for the specs for a 200-400 square foot home through a CAD (computer-aided design) program. During the students' seventh and eighth grade years, they would design along with the CTE teacher. In this way, they become part of the building project and learn alongside the builder. They would learn to read schematic diagrams, layout copper pipe to city code, wire for wall receptacles, as well as measure and fit cabinets for kitchens and plastic pipe for bathrooms.

It would also be exciting for each student to submit a design for a piece of multifunctional furniture that could also be added to the house. I imagine it could be a sustainable project in which the students auction or raffle the house off at the end of the school year and the proceeds go to funding the next year's house. Just imagine the training experiences students could carry with them into their future!

Students who were exposed to projects such as The Tiny House Project would be able to enter high school with a better idea of what industry they may want to focus on to prepare for the work world. They can begin with a much stronger idea of what they think they may want to do to be self-sufficient as an adult, but it would change as their curiosity and learning develops.

Middle school should begin with exploratory courses on business, entrepreneurship, and marketing. Experience and foundations in these three areas often lead students to develop projects that can produce future jobs. Throughout middle school, students need to experience many real-life projects. Each year, students need to apply for and shadow a client whose job interests them. When they get back to the classroom, they can share the story of the person they shadowed and share what captivated them (or not) about the job as a future prospect.

This is also the perfect time for *all* students to experience the "old school" four main home economics courses that high schools used to expose to students, not just cooking and sewing for girls and carpentry, and welding for boys. (Except today all students would take all four courses as life skills.) The idea is opening every drawer and toolbox in the house and learning how to use it. These skills may be everyday skills but can lead to further development in the future.

Schools should begin exploring students' interests around careers and skills in middle school. If your school or district doesn't have opportunities for students in this area, spearhead a collaborative effort between parents and teachers to change this.

Each short four-to-six-week course identifies tools and uses them, creating experiences that end with a project of the student's choice. The options are vast and varied such as: creating a dinner for four that might be used on a special occasion, sewing canvass sail bags for toting clothes or tools, creating a piece of furniture that can be multifunctional, or creating and cutting a sign logo using welding tools to put on their house or room. These projects not only provide skills but take applying math to a truly practical level.

These are just a few of the ideas that involve students in learning how to perform tasks while learning about the multiple job opportunities that evolve from acquiring skills. Explore the many career sites found on Google or listed through your state, like *www.californiacareers.info*.

Websites like these have fascinating lesson plans. There is a career surfer site that explores 1,000 career occupations. Many parents enjoy looking at these sites along with their children. In the wake of current industry layoffs, many parents are looking ahead to broaden their own futures as well.

There is a young man named Sam who creates canvass covers for boats. His business covers three different marinas in the San Diego area. Everyone wants his number because canvass erodes with the sun and winds, and storms tear them apart. His customers keep returning. One day I asked Sam how he got started.

"My mother sewed canvass for other people," he told me, "and they never paid her well. She said their business wasn't good at making the frames for the awnings and they would fall apart. I decided I would help her set up her own business until I found it was the most lucrative business in town. We became partners. My mom and I work fast, keep our fees reasonable, and make over $10,000 plus most months. I didn't dream of this as a career, but I'm now taking my eight-year-old son on most jobs to help and shadow me."

Back in the old days, people only saw women as cooks. Today, however, with the plethora of TV cooking shows, we find that many of the world's best chefs are men. Instead, many women often don a carpentry tool belt, especially on shows where creative people are flipping houses.

A master welder once told me they were looking to train women welders in the future. I interviewed two young girls who were welders and asked them how they got into the business. One girl said she was from a family of welders, her mother and father both made a good income. The other girl said she got in because of her dainty hands. A welder once told her that they had a great need for women to weld fine wires and get into tiny spaces. Most men's hands were just too big.

"I always wanted to be a jeweler," one of the girls said. "I figured if I first learned to do this kind work, I could learn to do the other. I was given an apprenticeship that paid more money than I ever dreamed of earning. So, I guess I'm going to stay with welding for a while, maybe I'll create jewelry as a side business." Like this young woman, many women fall into jobs when the opportunity presents itself.

Our students all need exposure to learning different skills which can also captivate a student's interest, especially in those impressionable years between ages eight and sixteen. If our schools are not encouraging things like shadowing your parent at work, shadowing jobs, participating in career days, or building summer apprenticeships, *you* as a parent should. It becomes the opportunity for a parent to create these experiences for their own children. I know quite a few dads who have their children work at their worksite paying them for on-the-job training.

11

Skillful Futures

"I give 98 percent of my mental energy to chess; others give only 2 percent."

~ BOBBY FISHER

Whether your child shadows ten people or just a few in middle school, each and every experience can be used later in life. I once had a father with three daughters tell me there was no way any of them would have a car license unless they could change a car tire themselves.

I have since thought of that dad's expectation when stranded on a road waiting for AAA.

Expectations are a good thing. I have always been of the mindset that if we don't have high expectations for our children's learning, we might as well have low expectations because most people fall short. I remember my teachers wanting to know *my* expectations for the school when I became their principal. I would always say, "I don't want this to be just a good school; I'm sure it already is. I want it to be a great school." We had to define together what great would look like by looking at other great schools and seeing how we could do it better. Not all were on board with that philosophy. To some, like many professions, good enough was enough.

If we were *just* good enough, the students would clearly get cheated. Keeping up with the future is a challenge for *all* schools today. You want to prepare students to be flexible, adaptable, and independent enough to adjust to each growing new trend.

We need to be building children's experiences in both **hard** and **soft skills** (before they leave middle school) to build their confidence with the grit to adapt. Suppose you are homeschooling your child and you are determined that your child gets to experience how to use every tool in your toolbox that is out in your shed. You set up projects with them to build a bird house. And perhaps you build some raised gardens for your vegetables. Then your child wants to design and build a clubhouse in the yard. You decide that you don't have enough experience yourself to build a shed from scratch, so you order a Tuff shed to be delivered to the yard. Together, you measure and place the dry wall, then build the shelves and benches to be added to the shed. Now your child has decided that they want electricity to run lights and internet, so you need a tradesman to come in. This presents the perfect opportunity for your child to learn from the pro (the electrician you bring in) who can show you how the wiring and receptacles can be brought safely into a pre-approved and safe space. Perhaps you will learn how to connect the system to a solar panel on the roof.

Any time you bring a tradesman to your house, it is a perfect chance for shadowing experience, and an added opportunity to interview the worker. Max, a friend's son, always took the opportunity to talk with any service worker who came to his house.

"So how many years have you been working at Stanley Steemer?" he asked the service professional.

"Six years," the man answered back.

"How much does someone who does work like you make an hour?" he asked.

"Well, in the beginning I used to make $18 an hour working for someone else" the man said. "But then I got my own truck and have my own satellite business. I work for a franchise company, and we share the profits. In two hours, we can make $500 to $1000 a house, depending on what they want done. I go 50/50 with the franchise company. I have even hired another man to train for $18 and hour. I make about $60 an hour for my time, but I have all the overhead. It gets me closer to making the payments on my own house."

After Max filled out the pros and cons in his notebook, I asked him if he thought this might be something he might consider for the future.

"No, I don't think so. There are a lot of business opportunities I can grow into for services, but I need to select something that has a high learning curve," he said. "Something that might take me years to learn and that I could never learn enough about. I don't want to get bored."

"Do you have any idea what that might be or look like?"

"Nope, I have no idea what it will be for me, but I'll know it when I find it. My friend is lucky. He wants to be a chef. You can never learn enough about being a good chef. There is so much to learn, not to mention managing a kitchen, and perhaps owning your own restaurant. That's where the real profit is."

"Would you ever want to do that?"

"No, I burn toast. I have no interest in learning how to prepare tastes. I just like to eat simple things."

I must say I felt my conversation that day with Max was impressive. By seventh grade, Max was well on his way to knowing so much about what he wanted and didn't want to do for a living. Exploring the work world is often an evolution in appreciating others and respecting how they grew into their career and what they needed to do to get there.

Another friend's son always wanted to be an actor. For the past fifteen years, he has worked hard in restaurants to maintain his lifestyle through tips. He has a portfolio and continues his craft knowing that unless he gets that prized role in a show, he won't make enough to buy a home and have a family in the Los Angeles area.

Many children grow up with dreams of singing, acting, or sports. It is their passion and their dream. They practice their craft daily and hope for that lucky break. We don't want them to let go of that dream. But suppose they had a skilled job that paid well, that they could do from home, and that could give them the flexibility to try out for roles or work on the side part time. That's what Harrison Ford did. Harrison Ford of *Raiders of the Lost Ark* and *Star Wars*, often shares how he was a self-taught carpenter for *many years* before getting cast as a lead actor.

Technology has opened many doors for careers in data processing, digital marketing, and advertising. These skills can become the bread and butter in people's lives as well as transferable skills to almost any other industry one might want to explore. Many businesses consider people who are adept at technology as highly valued employees.

When a person is interviewing you for a job today, most employers are asking about how good your computer skills are. This has become a major divide between the younger and older generations. People over a certain age weren't brought up accessing anything on computers like younger people are. Computer skills of any kind are highly regarded as a transferable skill. Almost every occupation needs someone to sort and store the data or access the apps and docs that run the business.

Hacking is something many industries need to be prepared for. Banks, border patrol, internet companies, FBI, airlines are looking for coders who have taken articulated courses in high school. Students who were on that robotics team and those who enjoyed those algorithmic experiences are being hired right out of high school. Some industries whispered on stage at a university workshop I attended that they particularly were looking for women because they could see design patterns in coding differently. Whether cybersecurity, coding, or any technology discipline, the more of these experiences our students have, the more they are valued.

As I mentioned before, my first school which had its second language challenges was labeled 'The Little Engine that Could' when it achieved a Distinguished School designation. The entire staff realized that reading many books was key to a growing vocabulary. We developed incentives like school shirts for students who earned twenty-five points, and if worn on Wednesdays it earned them the right to cut to the front of the line at recess and lunch.

However, if you earned over 100 accelerated reader points, this qualified the student to go camping with the principal at the end of the school year. Students worked arduously to achieve the right to go. For many an underprivileged youth, it was their first opportunity to go anywhere and the first time to be away from home. Our school's Teacher of the Year, a retired Marine, reserved a campground on Camp Pendleton for our group of well over 100 each year. On the last weekend of the school year, we left at 8:00 a.m. Saturday on a ninety-seat bus, and by 9:00 a.m. we were pitching tents with dozens of helpful Marines earning volunteer time.

Begin your work portfolio as early as middle school. Include your: shadow experience, mentorships, apprenticeships, internships, and work experience. Also add any volunteer hours you contributed to in your community.

The students split into groups of four and earned points for participation for skill building activities such as team building rope courses, crafts, fishing lakeside, building, orienteering, archery, and of course chess. It may have only been an overnight trip, but the experience was a lifetime of skills that many students may never have been exposed to. (Did I mention that almost all the staff freely volunteered giving *some* time to this awesome event?)

I recently had lunch with a friend who was a long time CTE teacher in our local high school. He had started an EdCorp (entrepreneurial learning) in 2016 with the students in his web design articulated credits class. I mentioned the word portfolio.

"Don't get me started on the word portfolio. It is so frustrating. There isn't a student in my class who understands what it is or what it should contain. Shouldn't the district be creating a way to have students capture all their work experiences somehow earlier than junior year of high school?"

I shook my head, "Yes, I believe that should begin in middle school. San Diego County schools have a method of creating badges toward work experience to place in district digital portfolios in some sixth grade classrooms. Many schools that have developed pathways have joined the 'Linked Learning Alliance". Imagine a pathway in your industry in which the English teacher and the mathematics teacher are helping the students focus on their own growth as they develop their skills in an industry of their choice. The English teacher would have students visit their digital portfolio each month, entering new job shadow opportunities, interviews, volunteer work, or work-related experience.

Essential hard skills are those that might enable us to perform the task (industry training); the **soft skills** are the valued skills that make us employable.

Essential soft skills are usually those your child has learned to develop in that first job. Talk with your child about the impact that first letter of recommendation is going to have on every other job they pursue. It is that respect the employer had for the employee's ability to value their position and perform it with a good attitude with respect for everyone around them that shows in recommendation letters. That first letter of recommendation from an employer needs to speak to all the recommended soft skills (see below).

A recent employer commented, "This generation of graduates always wants to start at the top. It seems the menial jobs are beneath them. Within a week they are calling in sick or consistently show up late." The reality is, if you want to impress your boss, show up early and be eager to learn more.

"Anything worth doing is worth doing well," was something my dad often taught me. This is *so* true. Whether you are placing items on shelves, cleaning the back room, or serving customers, you are serving your own time and that of others. Respect your time and theirs by doing it well.

Here is a list of vital **soft skills** recommended by the workforce industry:

- Respect for all people
- Show up on time (which usually means early)
- Good attitude
- Good communication skills
- Always ready to learn
- Be ready to take direction
- Be a team player

EXPERIENCE

To experience means to be enthusiastically involved, engrossed, enthralled, or really absorbed.

A middle school teacher received a grant to purchase three 3-D printers for the class.

"We are each going to create objects and toys that can be sold for the Annual Holiday Drive," said the teacher.

"Can we copy actual action figures?" asked a student.

"That is a great question," the teacher said. "No, you can't. That would be copyright infringement."

After a brief discussion on uniqueness and what constitutes a toy, students began drawing prototypes to fit the description of what makes their creation a toy, along with a description of its use.

12

Connecting to the Purpose of School

When I would walk through the district's schools as the Career Tech Consultant, one of the high school principals would often comment about the students. "I wish just once when I ask students why they were at school, they would tell me they wanted to get ready to get a good job."

The principal moved over to some students who recognized me as being their elementary principal. He went about asking each one, "Why did you come to school today?"

All of them answered, "To see my friends, of course."

One answered, "Well, I have tennis practice today."

The principal turned to me and said, "I guess I didn't do a very good job of making the better connections with the work world."

"Me neither," I replied. "These students attended my elementary school."

American schools traditionally give students the experience of school without making connections to *why* we need the skills, experience, and certifications we are supposed to be getting there. However, many new charter schools (public schools focused on themes or goals) and satellite micro-community schools are cropping up as a school of choice because they are preparing the students to learn at their own pace with the goal to develop their interest toward the work world.

Community schools are currently the big 'buzz' on television in California. Like Charter Schools and private schools, it calls for active parents to partner and volunteer time at the school. The four pillars are around the goal that children need to feel safe, engaged, and connected with opportunities for expanded learning time.

Whether it fits a formula for small K-8 or K-12 schools, most public elementary schools with an active parent community can create similar cultures.

Since the Pandemic, students have come back to school with challenging behaviors. It isn't just some schools it is in *most* schools. Generally, students have a shorter attention span, lack of self-control, and lack basic courtesy and respect for others. Whether this is caused by too much time on devices, violent video games, or lack of positive exposure to others, it is a large problem for teachers to redirect children to participate in cooperative learning activities.

Two district principals asked me what *one* thing I would try to change for the coming year if I were back leading a school. I quickly answered I would try to bring teachers and parents together to help **create a culture** of manners, respect, and kindness. This would begin with the teachers at the start of the new school year brainstorming what common language and expectations one should anticipate as manners and respect for everyone, in the classroom, on the playground, and everywhere else.

Once all the staff has *committed* to being on the same page it would be important to sign the parents up for supporting this life skill at home as well. If manners and respect are not occurring at home, bad behaviors transfer back into the school.

If we dream about what kind of school we want our children attending, it is the school where manners and respect are given top priority. This is one of *the top life essential skills* needed for employment. If we are serious about teaching the whole child and creating a culture around manners, respect, and kindness, it allows for everything else that is important to follow.

The second school I was assigned to was technically broken. The principal had been given a new school to open and had taken a good portion of her staff with her. The community was in an uproar, and the staff that remained were not happy. New staff were coming in the door each day and it was safe to say most people were not getting along. I knew this would take time to fix. After the first year of sheer survival, it was time for everyone to get on the same page and begin a process of creating a new school with a culture.

I was a science teacher in my previous life, so I asked the staff, "Does anyone know what a bar magnet is?" Everyone nodded yes. "Okay, does anyone know how you can break a bar magnet?" Everyone stared, and no one was game to answer. "It is quite simple. You only need to drop it on the floor. What happens then is all the ions scatter in a million directions leaving the magnet powerless and unable to attract or repel its positive and negative spheres to any magnetic material. The *only* way you can fix it is taking a stronger magnet and stroking the magnet for fifteen minutes in one direction, allowing for the ions to start facing in a positive direction again. I believe this is what happened to our school, and until we all agree to take a turn and face one direction, we cannot be effective.

We spent our first year setting up a lot of new systems for safety and other academic approaches, but creating a *culture* around what we all *value* is the only way we can be effective with creating bigger changes that we hope to add in the future. Peter Drucker, an industry manager once said, "Culture eats strategy for breakfast. It is the surest route to any organizations success."

This metaphor seemed to resonate with the staff. We decided on the goals of focusing on the three B's (Be respectful, Be responsible, and Be safe as our starting point, later adding Be Kind). I must warn new principals, directors, and staff that it takes about three years of consistency and effort to change the needle on building a culture. But trust me, the journey is worth the time. Everything else you hope to develop in your schools will happily follow.

13

Help Guide Student Interest

How can we help children understand why they go to school? The simple answer is, grab *every* opportunity for your children to learn what they have an interest in, then help them see themselves as more powerful with that knowledge. True learning only comes from *wanting* to learn more about a subject. Children know what their interests are, and they figure them out at an early age. They gravitate toward learning more about a topic themselves without our help.

In schools, this movement is called "child-centered curriculum." Teachers (and schools) have developed approaches that focus on the child exploring the answers to higher level questions through the lens of their own interest.

As parents, we can guide talks and help frame our children's experiences. If your children love music, dance, acting, painting, or sports of any kind, you look to feed their interests and see where it goes. When we see our children showing *genuine* talent, we have an obligation to *feed those experiences* for as long as they stay actively engaged.

For example, if you are traveling in the summer, consider exposing your children to the work world that surrounds them through the lens of experience. Have them interview museum docents, a camp supervisor, a head chef, as well as the manager of the hotel where you're staying. Have some discussion around full-time and part-time jobs and how people sustain their lifestyle.

Most young children have a natural curiosity. It's important to help them chase those internal questions. In elementary school, it is hard to feed them all. Elementary students love to try almost anything — *once.* They are testing their curiosity.

As principal of my second school, I suggested to the parents that I would like to bring as many of the experiences our community could supply to the school with an after-school program. At the time, I was a single mom struggling to get my boys to all the practices and teams they wanted to play on.

The community thought it was a great idea. We ran a small program every six weeks after-school in our first year of 2008. The Parent Teacher Organization (PTO) offered a one-day-a-week nominal fee for each program creating a couple of scholarships. For six weeks, students had access to programs such as: karate, dance, Mad Science, water painting, drama, robotics, and chess.

Parents and local artists were vetted into the program qualifying through a simple TB test and finger printing supporting the California "Megan's Law." By the end of the first three years, the school had a venue that housed close to sixty after-school programs throughout the year from hula dancing, sign language, etiquette, tennis, cooking, and organic farming.

I was hoping our public middle schools would continue to support student interest with skill camps. The truth was middle school students didn't need babysitting anymore. The only offerings that might keep students staying after school were a few sport programs, or possibly a YMCA program. Students usually went home to play video games without parental supervision until a guardian came home. Sadly, this is still true even today.

I'm also of the opinion that, when middle school students are at home for hours unsupervised, much can (and often does) happen. As an assistant principal of a middle school, I was always saying to parents, "We spend a lot of years paying for babysitters of elementary children when it is the middle school children who need the most supervision."

Middle school is a vital time for parents to nurture their children's interests. Some innovative parents have developed cohorts of four-to-six students who get together for interests after school and in the summers. I know of one group (cohort) who set up a summer of swimming lessons, Junior Lifeguard training, karate, guitar, and skateboard camps. The parents took turns shuttling the kids to different sites. These same parents set programs up during Covid-19 but saw the value of keeping the programs going after the stay-at-home orders ended. Certainly, the kids wanted it to continue.

These choices are a great start for a cohort summer school experience. But see if you can infuse some shadowing experiences for coding, band jam, or 3-D printing CAD programs. Help give your children exposure to other parents and their jobs. Visit a business or job center, shadow an adult, and interview them on what helped them get their job.

You can begin by asking your children what they might want to learn more about and then feed the frenzy of their curiosity. Consider asking a mom or dad to teach a week-long skill class like sewing a duffle bag on a sewing machine, building a chicken hutch, or building raised vegetable gardens.

This year, I had the privilege of visiting a chateau in Burgundy, France. It was a tour set up for a wine tasting paired with a family-style meal at this 12th Century picturesque castle hosted by the Count himself. The count led us through his 800-year-old residence that had housed twenty-eight generations of family members surviving war and insurrection that span its survival through the French Revolution, WWI, and WWII.

The castle was in some disrepair, but the Count and family were obliged to continue the legacy of the family into the future. Without any assistance from the government, the family oversees the winery, wine tours, and hosts weddings, and other special events weekly at the chateau. What impressed me most was the work ethic, manners, and warm personality of his three school-aged sons who assisted in delivering the casserole of Boeuf Bourguignon to the tables, greeting the guests, as well as the cleaning of the tables after the meal. I thought to myself, if a Count has no problem creating experiences for his younger sons on how to create sustainable incomes to support the chateau, why aren't the rest us preparing our children with authentic work experiences that will serve their future? Training his sons to be vested in the family business created expectations and invaluable social skills to prepare them for any future jobs.

14

What are Pathways?

"The winner of the game of chess
is the person who makes the least mistakes."

~ SAVIELLY TARTAKOVER

In the past five years, community colleges and four-year institutions have moved to pathway systems. These pathways give training through consecutive courses that align with an industry.

If a student begins showing interest in computers, health and medicine, digital marketing, engineering, or one of two dozen more industries, they can access the articulated credit courses in high school Career Technical Education (CTE) courses. These courses not only help students realize the different careers that are available through that industry, but also help them design the path to get there.

Schools that are in their initial development phase of pathways usually have two sequence courses one in their junior and one in senior year. More developed schools have three and four years of industry courses. That means a student can have three or four industry courses completed before they enter college.

A generation ago, you may remember public schools pushing "college for all students," with the argument that degrees would lead to high-paying jobs. Unfortunately, there was a gap. Colleges were not aligning course work with what industries needed as skills for hiring. So, the fate of those who spent four or more years in college (not to mention tens of thousands of dollars) was that often their degrees could not get them a job.

Many students with liberal arts degrees moved back in with their parents, trying to return to community college or trade schools and become certified in *any* industry that was hiring. But the high schools that began offering pathway career courses researched the industries within twenty miles of their base. Studies show that most people do not move far away from their family, friends, and hometown.

Some towns had biochemical companies taking root, shipping businesses, hospitality industries for tourism, car manufacturing (which was becoming digital and electrical). And of course, large industries like Amazon and Fed Ex are starting to have robotics and data driven industries within them.

The long and short of things is this: courses that used to be for trade jobs (now referred to Career Tech CTE) are now needed for most jobs. Many students are still coming out of high schools uncertain about what they want to get into for a career. But luckily, many of the CTE courses they took (or will take) have transferable skills to many industries.

Suppose you are in high school, and you take a CTE coding class, a digital design class, and combine it with a marketing, business, or and engineering class. All these are articulated classes. That means if you earned a 'B' or better, this course will be accepted as credits in most colleges today. In many cases today if you receive an 'A', it will be calculated into your college GPA grade point average. In the past it was only the AP courses that were transferable. But now, it is the career courses that are sought after. Why? Because those (CTE) courses often lead to today's higher wage jobs and careers. Public education is *finally* connecting school to the work world. Currently, because of the severe shortage of licensed skilled workers, the demand for skills is great, and so are the hourly wages.

Most industries are willing to train eager, interested, and reliable students. Many of these career opportunities *start* at $50 an hour. If a student didn't earn an internship in high school, they can try again in community college, or (in some cases) pay for the internship themselves. My youngest son paid Apple for his internship training. A successful internship often secures the participant a guaranteed job. He has successfully worked for Apple over thirteen years.

It makes sense that, if we are truly a country that stands behind college and career readiness, we should prepare everyone to at least get certified to start in some industry of their interest when they leave school. Students learning something they love from an early age is a great "why" to continue learning.

How do parents engage shadowing, apprenticeships, and internships? These terms are confusing. One career tech teacher had his engineering class shadow (spend a day) with a recent start-up 3-D design business in a newly developed industrial park in Carlsbad, California. The business was small enough to show the progression between the designs the engineers needed to create, the computer programs they needed to set up, and the manufactured objects that needed to be packaged. They shipped goods to many other American companies.

It was very interesting to see the elaborate array of bits and pieces ordered from bolts and frames to toys and furniture. Once the designs were created by CAD programs, the plastics were fed by ribbons of plastic to create whatever shape and size the product needed to be. Many middle and high school engineering classes had 3-D printers in their classrooms, so our students were intrigued and engaged. At that time, there were multiple 3-D printing companies springing up in the area. The students also recognized that, as future designers and engineers, they could work with different items using the same core concepts. In one career, they would use engineered concrete for creating houses, and in another, cellular matter for creating transplant organs. The students asked wonderful questions. They learned how many people worked on a team, how many people the company employed, and what kind of education a prospective employee needed.

When we got back to the classroom, however, the excitement turned toward going home and other plans. I felt the teacher missed an opportunity to spend some discussion time around what the students saw and what they experienced. How did they all process the visit? How many of the students might see themselves working for this little company in the next town?

That little company may not have appealed to everyone, but students considering and then sharing the pros and cons of careers from their perspectives is something we do not develop enough at home or in most classrooms. When I asked the teacher if he felt it might be a conversation for the future, he was honest and said "No." He told me, "I don't have the time in my school day."

If we don't talk about the work world in school, where does that conversation happen?

I began interviewing the students about their idea of a career. At the time, I was working on developing pathways in high schools. This teacher had established a two-sequenced pathway. During the first course, the students would take architecture. In the second course, they took engineering. Unfortunately, there was a disconnect causing the pathway to fail before it could properly germinate in the students. The counselors were still calling the courses electives and the students who were now in the second course did not know they were in a pathway program. The counselors never explained it, the teacher certainly didn't, and students didn't have a clue what a pathway was, or how it could benefit them.

I had my work cut out for me, because the students didn't even know that getting over a 'B' grade in those so-called (CTE) electives gave them transferable college credits. They had preliminary engineering course credits in most college pathway programs and were completely ignorant of that fact.

I had a conversation with one student who was planning to join the Marines. Camp Pendleton was near their hometown of Oceanside, California.

"Did you know that the Marines have pathways built into their programs?" I said to that student.

"No," he replied, "I'm still not sure what that is myself."

"Well, let's say you have two pathway courses in design and engineering. And you have an interest in learning more. The Marines need to make parts for all forms of machinery and may have an interest in developing your interests throughout your career as a Marine. The armed forces try to match one's interest with their organization and will often pay for more training and the education. After you either step out of the Marines or retire, you're going to want to work at something. I am sure you are going to want a good-paying job for all your skills, training, and expertise."

Perspective shared with others often adds a lot of value.

I shared a story about a Marine who explored the value of testing elevators. His research showed him how each elevator in any military facility needed to be tested every year for safety. After putting in his time in the service, he would be fully licensed and would be one of the few who could make five hundred to a thousand dollars a day as an independent contractor qualified by the military to certify elevators in military institutions (of which there are thousands.) With a little research, he made quite a career for himself. I told the student that, if he used the pathway program, he could set himself up to be financially strong and happy with his career choice, even just out of high school.

American schools are beginning to develop sequence course work that aligns with the interests of the student in an industry. By the end of middle school, students are expected to choose a pathway of interest. It doesn't mean students can't change their minds at any point along the way.

By sophomore year, most students begin an industry course. Let's say your child selects computer coding. At the end of that year, if they share that the course was too linear for them and they are seeking something more artistic, they can switch to another pathway next year.

"Why don't you consider Digital Marketing?" the counselor may ask. "Marketing utilizes a lot more designing and artistic acuity. You already have enhanced your computer skills."

Career programs like pathways may also try to give students the opportunity to shadow a person with a business in town during a weekday or in the summer. If a student takes a real interest in the work, they may be able to apprentice at that business the next year. There are a lot of options, and more are popping up. (Some high schools with pathways have students working or interning within the industry in their senior year.)

Pathways are the wave of the future, especially in California. There are some states that do exploratory industry training in middle school. Career industry pathways capture early experiences for students to introduce them to the skills and working environment before they graduate high school. The icing on the cake is they are earning college credit before they enter college. In these middle schools, students are expected to shadow people for a day several times a year throughout middle school. As early as eighth grade, students can begin an apprenticeship for a week or more with a company who will expose the students to real working environments. This boots-on-the-ground experience develops the soft skills students will need to get hired after they stop attending school as well as a peek at the environment surrounding the workspace.

The objective of public education is for *all* students to have equal access to higher-paying jobs. Districts are slowly developing Career Technical Education (CTE) pathways that align with the fifteen main industry sectors. High schools in most localities look at the industry jobs that are housed nearby and produce the most accessible jobs for students. Many districts develop their first pathway around health science and medical technology because of the number of accessible jobs and the large range of accessible careers that can lead to good paying jobs in most localities.

Educators are beginning to discuss that students as early as fourth and fifth grades should be given the RIASEC (Realistic, Investigative, Artistic, Social, Enterprising, and Conventional) quiz to begin the talks around their interests and personalities.

Research says most students will have a dozen jobs or more in their future and about 65% of students will own their own business either part-time or full time because they *can* in the digital world. It makes sense for established industries to pave the way for their young to grow within their state. It also makes sense to start preparing students for industry jobs while taking some of the course work in high schools. *Nothing* is lost in how you develop yourself.

There is no doubt that engaging students in simulated work situations and having them learn the skills they will need for careers in the real world keeps them more connected to the why of going to school.

Pathways create a school within a school climate. Ideally, this would begin in middle school, then carry on into high school cohorts of students who travel together and grow within an interesting industry sector. This model gives students work opportunities and networking possibilities for their futures.

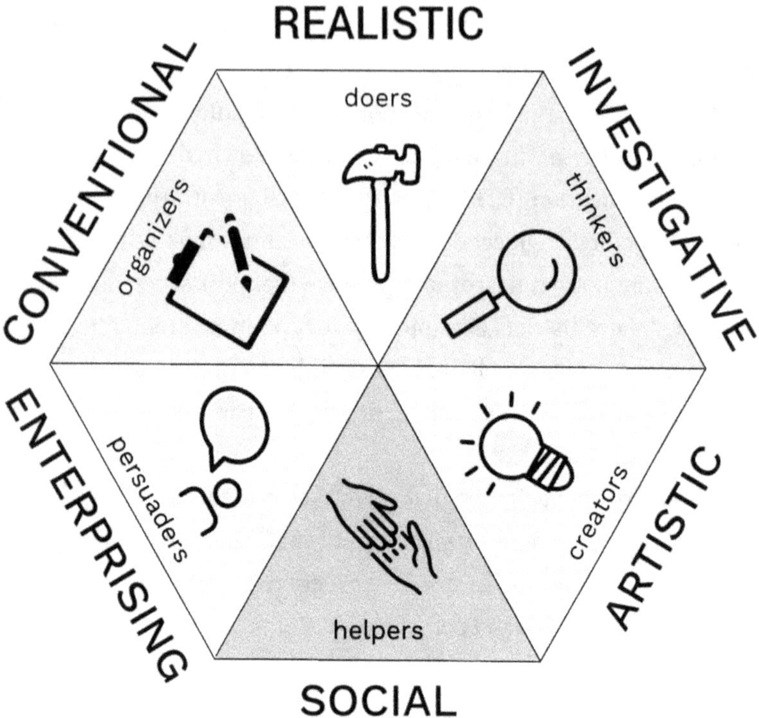

The RIASEC framework uses six themes to describe people's interests and match them with careers.

When a person's work environment fits their interest themes, they are more likely to perform better at work, achieve greater academic and career success, and may even earn more money than their peers.

The six RIASEC themes are arranged in a hexagon — the letters next to each other have more in common than the ones farther away. They are also sometimes called "Holland Codes." Most people claim a combination of 2 or 3 themes.

Some people's interests change as they get older and sometimes they don't change at all. You know your own likes and dislikes the best, so it's up to you!

https://workforce.org/san-diego-jobs/my-next-move-2/riasec/

15

Shopping for Schools

For the past century, selecting a school environment wasn't an option as much as it is today. You and your parents grew up in a community and usually went to the nearest school. If you were picky, you might have specifically moved to be closer to the school you felt would be a good fit for your child's education or placed them in a private school.

Much has changed in the past ten years.

The digital world has been the catalyst for this changing landscape as some students can learn remotely and others need more specialized themes to hold their child's attention. As our children become more social, we begin to expand our search for schools that may best accommodate our children's needs and interests.

Public schools offer some state-funded preschool beginning at the age of three. But that is mostly for students who display delays in speech and language or other disabilities. Most states currently offer free preschool or T-K (Transitional Kindergarten) beginning at the age of four and Kindergarten part/full day at five. There are also federally funded grants for preschool academies in many of our lower socioeconomic neighborhoods. These academies have been taking the place of the Head Start programs from days gone by. Whether your child begins school at three or six is something you can decide based on your child's needs.

This ability for parents to choose when their child is ready for school has been a long time coming. School wasn't mandatory in most states until the age of six. However, research data was clearly showing that children needed to be reading independently at their grade level by third grade. Despite added reading programs supported mostly by Federal Title 1 Funds, the graduation rate continued to decline over decades. And the independent reading rate became more challenging to fix. It made sense to create *free* access to preschool programs that would prepare children to read earlier.

For those who can afford private schools, there are many which support specialized programs or religious beliefs. Other early educational experiences that continue to increase in popularity are the Waldorf and Montessori Schools. Both early 20th century philosophies appealed to parents who wished to develop the whole child as a lifelong learner.

Waldorf Schools were created by Rudolf Steiner, and focus on the philosophy of head, heart, and hands. It is a non-academic approach in the early years which proposes children should first develop imagination and fantasy. This type of school focuses on a child's imagination and artistic expression, often bringing in mathematics first and moving onto reading and writing in first and second grade.

Montessori Schools were introduced by Maria Montessori, an Italian physician. She opened her first school, Casa dei Bambini, in an underserved community of Rome in 1907. The school introduced the basics in preschool, usually starting from grades three through six. Montessori allows students to gain knowledge through hands-on learning. Students have free choice based on their interests to work independently and to accomplish experiential tasks.

Often, parents opt for public or charter schools as their kids begin their first experience with school. The price is right (free), and they may have moved to the neighborhood for that purpose. Most parents need to work, and public schools can also offer before and after care programs.

Community Schools (also free) serve over twenty-five million students in mostly underprivileged areas. Their mission is to bring together parents, teachers, and community resources such as health care, tutoring, counseling, and extended after school programs to service the whole child. The goal is to help students overcome their barriers and help them become successful in life suppling academic growth and developing *life skills*. One of the most prestigious community schools in San Diego is the Monarch school for homeless students. It supports over 300 students K-12 and has the assistance of many influential organizations.

> *Shopping for a Middle School and High School should be tied more to the interests of your child and the industry they want to learn more about.*

It is my personal belief that all schools should develop the model of community schools focusing on building culture and yearly goals in partnership with the teachers, parents, and community to support all students' success.

Regardless of your school choice, parents will need to be vigilant from the start about how their children are adjusting to the new school environment. If they are having trouble adjusting (falling behind and feeling isolated) it may be time to meet with your child's teacher. Remember, you are your child's best advocate, and no one knows your child better than you. Frustrated children halt their natural curiosity and growth process, which can impact the socio-emotional development of a child. It may be that the school is not a good fit for them.

Active parenting is the key to your child's success. A one-size school doesn't fit all. Today, you have a lot more ability to choose a school that best fits your child's learning style and interest.

The Pandemic caused a nationwide spike in parents exploring home-schooling as an option. One local paper, during those lockdown weeks, advertised an evening for parents to learn more about homeschools. That night, the public library was full of curiosity seekers. Some parents felt their children needed a more hands-on curriculum and the present distance learning model wasn't working for their child because they were falling further behind. Homeschool parents seemed to have the inside track on where other parents could buy support materials. That night, they shared that on average homeschool parents spent close to $2,000 for basic curriculum support materials.

Yet, these parents shared many reasons for creating their own home-school experience. One parent shared how her child was reading at a third-grade level in kindergarten. That parent wanted him to be paced to his learning ability. Another parent said their child had special needs and felt more one-on-one was needed for their child. Another parent stated she hated the "pack" mentality schools often promoted.

"My child began to shut down by second grade," she said. "She was being bullied by groups of girls who didn't want to play with her or be near her because she was shy."

A parent asked me what I thought about transferring their fourth-grade child to a homeschool environment. I advised them to include the child in the decision. Why? If you don't, the child will perceive any negative aspects as something done to them, not something they chose to do. Always have children vested in their future.

Public school curriculum, despite naysayers' protests, keeps pace to cover the average student. Teachers spend time each day supporting the lower-level student's ability to catch up, while providing more challenging options for students who are further ahead. It is a juggling act to be sure. Most teachers will affirm they have barely enough time to get the day's work done. When measuring the amount of time for any one child to perform the same tasks at home with a parent, the performance tasks can be completed in a much shorter period of time allowing more extra-curricular time. Each school location, size, type, cost, etc. comes with pros and cons.

Today, educational theorists believe much more efficient and quality education can be obtained through learner-centered projects and curriculum. Many new schools crop up yearly focusing on such topics as music, art, and sciences. The trick is parents need to get their children to these schools each day.

In a first-grade classroom a child centered curriculum might look like a student fixated on big-rig trucks choosing to learn more about the truck's history and creating a timeline of how trucks changed over time based on what they needed to do and where they needed to go. They could also use the internet to research the big changes coming in the future for trucks. This theme can run through the world of math, constructing questions around travel time and distance. It can work in language arts, writing, etc. and personalized teaching can happen in smaller groups or home school settings.

In the past ten years, many communities chose to give public schools (especially districts with declining enrollment) a new look by creating a common theme or focus. Some schools developed themes around the performing arts. Others chose engineering STEM or STEAM schools (Science, Technology, Engineering, Arts, and Mathematics Schools.) All focused specialty schools expect large parent involvement and participation.

If you live near a STEM school, usually you would automatically be accepted into that school. However, if you lived outside of its boundaries, you needed to apply through the District Office for a 'school of choice' application. Some schools such as High Tech High are so popular that all students, whether they live in the immediate boundaries or not, must apply through a lottery system.

There is always a window parents needed to pay attention to in the spring. But often these sought-after spots are run on a lottery system and may have a waiting list for students to get in.

Preparing for the transition to middle school can be especially stressful for parents. Students can't wait for the passage into middle school, but parents usually dread it. Most public-school districts herd students from many schools into one larger school. Class sizes go up, new friends are made, and there is a new pecking order of students clustering into groups. They share the same kind of interests (something to the effect of the old cliché "Birds of a feather flock together"). Most private schools keep the classes small through the eighth grade.

Many middle school students do not connect to the meaning of *why* they are there except to discover their teenage world of likes and dislikes among peers.

If you were really pleased with your child's elementary experience, you will want to make sure your middle school choice is a good fit for your child as well. Does it give experiences and opportunities in school and after school to develop their interest in growing life skills and industry sectors? Again, if your school is not providing these opportunities, it will up to the parents or cohort of parents to provide these valuable experiences.

It is in middle schools we often miss the chance to introduce much needed LIFE skills. Some schools rotate courses in six-week rotations. These skill opportunities can transfer across interest, careers, or side hustles such as:

- welding
- connecting pipes
- manipulating electrical systems
- culinary/cooking
- illustrating children's books
- horticulture/gardening
- working on car engines
- designing clothing
- crafting woodwork

In other words, middle school can give students experiential moments to learn how things work directly from someone who knows how to do it. Finding a middle or high school may not be as simple as following the predetermined plan that it is in your child's neighborhood. How well is the school doing at connecting students to real work experiences?

Walking into high school with an idea of what industry you want to focus on keeps students connected to the purpose of school and work. People evolve and so do students. They can begin with an idea of what they think they may want to do to be self-sufficient as an adult, but it changes as their curiosity and learning interest develop.

This is where parents can partner with their young adults to research and apply for high school programs that will serve the work world learning, and the other youth activities desired. Emerging into high school with skillful experiences from middle school then creates strategic focus of narrowing one's industry pathway selection, and this will benefit your child's future!

16

The Eight Keys to Success

"Openings teach you openings. Endgames teach you chess."

~ STEPHAN GERZADOWICZ

I worked in a school district that focused on *The Eight Keys of Excellence* by Suzanne LaFleur. At the time, our superintendent felt passionately that if the 18,000 students in our district understood those keys, they might have a better grasp on how to be successful in life.

In both my schools, I had a daily morning assembly. The bell rang, and all 800 students lined up in a horseshoe around the flag and recited *The Pledge of Allegiance*. We followed it with our four-lined school pledge which had been developed by one of our teachers. After that, we shared any necessary announcements. This was followed by repeating the eight keys with hand actions that supported the words. The entire event took about twelve minutes. But there we forged a connection between the students, the principal, and the community each morning. No matter how hot or cold, a student felt easier seeing his best friend was at school that day, that the principal had a face, and their teacher, their rock was there as their guardian for the day. Some weren't supportive, saying it wasted school time. But the community loved it as it reassured the parents that their children made it to school safe and a safe environment was there for their children.

I know what you're thinking; *How can a parent walk away any day and feel that kind of safety any more with so many shootings in the news?* I was a principal during Columbine and a principal during Sandy Hook. But the morning ritual created a rhythm every parent and every teacher and student knew and trusted. And as for the shootings, I took drills of all kinds seriously to ensure the safety of the students, faculty, and staff. It trained everyone for quick responses which is the best one can do in most given circumstances.

Repetition of the keys at each assembly did leave a memorable mark on each student. But did they really know what they meant? Teachers were given the keys to post in classrooms. Each month, the district focused on one of the eight keys. Some schools even created citizenship awards for students who were the best example of that month's focus key. LaFleur's book (and her audiobook) have been on the bestseller's list for years. I often had conversations with elementary students around the top key of Integrity when they visited me in my office.

"What do you think integrity is?" I asked a second-grade student one day.

"I don't know," he said. "Something that's good for you."

"In what way is it something that is good for you?"

"I'm not sure but it's the top key."

I tried to relate it to myself and speak to the student in a way they might relate as well.

"Well, I find it is something I *need* to work on every day because most days I'm being tested on it, especially the part that tells us, "Do I *mean* what I say and say what I *mean*."

"What does that mean exactly?" asked the seven-year-old boy who liked to use a lot of adverbs.

"Well, what does it mean when I say to you, you're a man of your word."

"It means I always keep my promise?"

"Yes, great, so when you said to your friend today, I'll meet you for a game of tetherball and didn't show up, what does that mean? If your actions speak to you valuing your friendship with people, how important was it for you to show up?"

"Important, I guess. But I forgot."

"So, it is one of those things we must work on every day. We know who we are: somebody who is honest, trustworthy, and can be relied on. But we get tested on our values most days, and if we keep to that old saying 'I'll treat others like I want them to treat me,' it works, doesn't it?"

"So how did that friend feel when you never showed up?"

"Sad."

"Probably," I told him. "Maybe he thought you didn't like him enough. It may not have been your intention, but he certainly didn't feel valued. You said he felt *sad*. And he had to carry that feeling around *all* day."

"Like I said, none of us are perfect, but to be a person who has integrity, we need to show how we value things every day. So, it becomes important when we value a friend to keep our word."

For most parents, this may be your first acquaintance with the eight keys. It certainly was mine when the superintendent brought them to our summer workshop that year. He shared how just being intimate with the keys changed other school districts and, as leaders of schools, he hoped we could encourage our staff to support it.

LaFleur outlines the eight keys in the following order:

1. **Integrity:** Align your actions with your values.

2. **Failure Leads to Success:** See failures as your feedback, each failure is a lesson.

3. **Speak with good purpose:** Be *positive* with your language.

4. **This is it!** Mindfulness, be present in the moment.

5. **Commitment:** Finish what you start, and what you set out to do.

6. **Ownership:** Take responsibility for your actions; do not blame someone else.

7. **Flexibility:** Adjust your sails to the wind and alter a course if it needs to change.

8. **Balance:** Feed your life with ways to enjoy the journey. Make time to be happy.

Last month, I was with a couple who were unpacking a car from a vacation and some very important items had been left behind. It happens. The three small children were sitting in the back of the car listening to a loud, aggressive argument ensuing around the box of vitals left behind.

Drop the seeds and grow the experiences that you all can share along the way. Be lifelong learners. Share skills and wisdom, because the future promises to take the "Jacks" and "Jills" of all trades on the ride of their lives.

"I had to pack every single thing for this trip and left it for you just to put in the car," said the mother.

"Well, I packed every single item that was left beside the car. *You* must have forgotten to put it downstairs by the car," blamed the dad.

"I did put every single box down there! But you got so busy putting in all these toys you forgot the critical box. You probably ran out of the room and just decided to leave the box."

The couple continued blaming each other for a few more minutes until they finally resigned themselves to the fact that they would need to live without the important items and be flexible.

But we certainly are our children's best teachers, good or bad. We model it for them. Later in the day, the three children began to cause a ruckus, arguing over whose fault it was that the playing cards didn't make it on the trip. Later, something got knocked off a table and they all blamed each other for the accident instead of the one who caused it owning up to it saying, "Sorry, my bad. I turned too fast, and it fell."

How much easier was it to *own* a problem? Everyone can move on from it, rather than never taking ownership and blaming everyone but themselves for an action. Ownership is so intrinsically tied to integrity. It speaks to action. People admire actions to values. Saying a quick phrase like "**Sorry, my bad!**" moves the disagreement off the table.

The couple didn't realize that, despite all their good intentions of teaching values to their children, their actions spoke so much louder than their words. It's a bit of a cliché, but still true. No matter which way we look at it, we are always teaching our children through our actions.

The eight keys have a plethora of hidden messages that relate to daily life lessons. In the future, flexibility will be a critical component for children to be successful in life. Jobs skills will certainly be changing as more people flood the market. One's ability to adapt a skill another way may win the day. At some point, they may have two or three businesses in their life running at the same time. One may take off, facing one with the question — do I fold the other business, or sell it off?

After we introduced the keys in school, we reminded ourselves when we missed the message. For instance, to be able to enter another country, you must complete a ten-page handout online. If you mess up one of the numerous panels for numbers, the application is thrown out, making it impossible to move forward without starting the entire process over again. "Failure Leads to Success" comes to mind here. I have no choice but to start it again or I can't enter the country, so what did I learn and where did I go wrong so I don't have to begin it a third time? Sounds a bit like losing at chess and learning from it.

Whether we want to believe it or not, when we become parents, we have signed up for a lifetime as continual teachers of children. The job will never be over. At times, we will make mistakes. But it is our most important job as parents to keep trying. So, seize the moment every day. This is it.

17

The Art of Courageous Conversations

"Good positions don't win games, good moves do."

~ GERALD ABRAHAMS

We often shy away from challenging, uncomfortable conversations with our children. They often catch us off guard and we haven't prepared arguments to discuss things logically. Learning as much as we can from as many as we can to be a life-long learner is going to take a village.

Just yesterday, I was standing in a line to pay at a register. I was listening to a mother talking to her demanding daughter. The daughter was about eight years of age and clearly a handful. After the mother had refused the daughter several requests to buy her items at the register, the little girl shifted her demands. She began asking why she needed to go to school. My ears perked up to listen to the mother's response.

"I hate school," said the girl (let's call her Dawn). "I don't see why I have to go. The teacher is stupid, I hate the kids in my school, and I already know everything they are trying to teach me, so why do I have to go?"

"Don't ask me why. You just have to go," said the mother.

"No, I don't," Dawn said. "I can learn everything on the computer. I don't need to go to the stupid old school."

"Well, you just have to, it's the law. You have to go to school until you graduate high school."

I lowered my eyes. *Wrong answer*, I thought to myself. You are passing the blame to a system and not establishing a compelling reason why we need to be exposed to all types of learning to be ready for the future.

I stood in line, hoping the mother wasn't going to give away her power in that precious moment. However, I also understood it wasn't a good time to get into the reasons for learning (and the best way isn't always from a computer). It would have been best to say we should discuss this later because it was too important a topic to discuss while shopping.

The mother could have taken a pause and said, "I want to hear more about why you are unhappy with school. We may have to consider another school or another type of school that will help you enjoy the learning process better."

I will always recall a speaker I had invited to my school to talk to parents, specifically fathers, who were often removed from meaningful conversations with their children due to work and other commitments. The speaker was a well-known district principal who had lost his youngest son three blocks from our school on the evening of the Christmas concert. His son, Danny, was a young police officer who would patrol our surrounding streets day and night. Unfortunately, it was a troubled area for gang activity.

On this harrowing evening, Danny was called to assist a female officer who had pulled a car over for a traffic violation. As he stepped out of his car to walk over to the car in question, a high-powered scope rifle fired a shot from a nearby yard. The bullet hit a fateful blow to Danny just under his bulletproof vest just under his arm. This was a shocking blow to our entire community.

It struck home to all of us at the school that young officer Danny (husband and father of a two-year-old), who was assigned to keep our streets safe, was fatally wounded by one of our own former students. The suspect later admitted he felt he would get a higher ranking in the gang if he killed a cop. Principal Steve Bessant stood in front of a filled audience facing parents anxious to hear from a man who would no longer be able to talk with his own beloved son. Steve is a humble man, often humorous, and he knew whatever his message would be on this evening, he could hit the hearts of a caring community.

"I'm not here to sadden our hearts with the story of my son's passing. Rather, I want to fill your hearts and souls with stories of the valuable talks I had with my sons in my car every day," Steve shared, adjusting the microphone. "These little treasured moments were like gifts raining in from the heavens in our hectic lives." The audience leaned forward and nodded their heads.

"I will always recall endless questions from both my sons about where babies came from." (You could hear the audience snicker). "We would travel from practice to practice talking about the Chargers and the Padres and, of course, how I decided on becoming a teacher after working many years as a chef in the Coast Guard. 'Well,' I said to them, 'I decided I really wanted to do something that mattered.'"

"My sons would throw questions out to me, and I would always throw one back to them. 'So, what kind of job do you feel might be a good *fit for you*?' I gradually began to realize the power of getting honest answers from someone was all in the question. If they weren't in a talking mood that day, as teenagers usually aren't, I would start, 'Hungry?' That would *always* elicit a response."

Steve continued, "You know you have about five good years of safe conversations with your kids in a car. A pastor once shared with us at church that people feel more relaxed when they were sitting side-by-side instead of across a table. He shared that eye-to-eye contact and in-your-face conversations just never seem as safe."

The conversations about what you want to be when you grow up seem to stop after elementary school. But it needs to *step up* and occur more frequently in middle school and high school. Instead of asking kids what they want to be, change it to what they can imagine themselves *doing*. We need to consider preteens as emerging adults and ask what industry they seem interested in pursuing.

By middle school, more serious conversations need to occur around what they want to learn more about. You could learn this, as mentioned in a previous chapter, by taking the online twenty-minute RIASEC test. The RIASEC gives scenarios that tap into our children's interest and personalities.

The best approach when you have some alone time with your children, which Steve so brilliantly pointed out, is using the hours we have in cars for asking good questions.

"So, you seem excited working on projects with your hands," you may ask. "Would you be interested in learning how to frame some buildings with a buddy of mine next summer? Perhaps we can find a cabinetmaker you can learn from for a week. Let's explore what you like or don't like about it. How does that sound?"

The last thing we want to do is have the same boring conversation that shuts everything down. You know, the ones that go like this:

"How was school today?"

"Fine"

"What did you do?"

"Nothing special."

We want to plant seeds for growing interest, especially any interest that can produce a skill they can use in the future.

"I'm going to try to landscape the yard better so we can use it as a living space. I've asked a professional for ideas. Would you like to sit in on that meeting with me? I'd enjoy your ideas. I wonder how much he makes for a living. He is asking for $500 for a quick drawing and an estimate. Does that seem interesting to you at all?"

If you are not sure how to begin conversations that can lead to in depth conversations, you can always start with the phrase "I wonder."

I was speaking with some first and second grade students in a car once. Halloween was coming soon and, of course, the first question I asked them was who or what they were dressing up as. This answer is always a favorite. It is an answer they have thought long and hard about.

"Mario," says one.

"Really? Why Mario?"

"Well, I play Mario every day, and I'm sick of being a superhero. That's kid stuff."

I tried an "I wonder" scenario. By seven years old, they see themselves as maturing. So, I pondered aloud.

"I wonder if there is going to be a full moon on Halloween?"

"Of course," says the seven-year-old.

I muse for a minute, "I don't think so."

"What — are you a mind reader?" asks the boy.

"Naw, I saw the moon last night. It was a waxing crescent moon." The former science teacher in me is always asking questions that can lead to deeper understanding around what we see and what we understand. The curiosity about "waxing crescent" could take the conversation to a glorious place. And it did.

I mused to myself. *Every kid knows what he wants to be for Halloween, but many have no idea what type of job would interest them in the future.*

Before that ride was finished, I had him look up the phases of the moon on Google and we began talking about what phase the moon would be on Halloween.

It took courage to go "down the rabbit hole" with those kids. It takes courage every day to be a *present* parent. We all need to keep learning how to perform skills differently for the rest of our lives. We will often need to seek qualified experts to help us. I need to do that every year for my job. Acquiring new skills will never stop. Sometimes the acquisition takes courage. Every moment is a teachable moment.

Tough love is tough on parents. It is those courageous conversations with your children and agreed upon expectations that are part of the job of parenting. All too often we become enablers, someone who continues to support the wrong behavior.

This book encourages parents not to fight children's battles for them. Developing resilience and grit is again a *skill* needed in adulthood. The earlier the child grasps the concept, the easier, the more complex issues become to solve.

For all the parents who read and share the contents of this book, know the future is brighter with the knowledge and experiences we provide our children with today. Remember we want our children to be able to live and sustain a happy future as independent adults, preferably enjoying their work world doing things that they love.

As parents it will be important to provide those experiences and have expectations for your children.

One mother I spoke to at the end of 2021 threw her hands up in the air.

"My son's high school gave him a high school diploma."

"That's good, isn't it?"

"No," she said, "because he didn't deserve it. Yes, he took the courses. Yes, he logged into the attendance for the class. But he never did *one* assignment. I kept telling him he would never graduate, and they just gave him a diploma anyway. I'm frustrated. I told him he just received his luckiest break in life."

"Yes, the schools are trying to deal with this Pandemic crisis. So, what are you going to do?"

"He needs to figure it out. It's up to him now."

"Are you expecting him to do something now, or is he just living comfortably at home? Because we know anyone who is comfortable isn't going to move on to anything."

"No, he's not on *my* couch. He moved into his girlfriend's house. He is eighteen."

"So, chances are he'll be back. Then what?" She shuddered and shook her head.

This conversation with a friend is hard and it is even harder for a parent with a child. What are you going to do with your life? Everyone must start somewhere. In a sea of missing skilled workers, it is a no-brainer. Go to a community college or trade school for almost nothing in cost and become licensed in a skill you would enjoy learning more about. A skill is never lost and will always be there for your plan B or C if you need it.

18

Life is a Chess Game

"The most powerful weapon in chess is to have the next move."

~ David Bronstein

A few years back, I became an Impact Teacher in a low socio-economic school near the border of California and Mexico.

By that time, there had been three different principals who had come through the door in a very short time frame, and the most recent principal came from Colorado. I was teaching remedial reading to the fifth and sixth graders, whose behavior was beyond challenging. It was a struggling school where student behaviors hadn't been addressed for years.

The students wanted to just play games on the district laptops for rewards, trying to convince me that the game of Fortnite taught people all the skills of life.

"No," I told them. "As a reward, I'm going to teach you the real game of life — chess."

They were a tough audience and weren't buying the idea of learning chess. *Not entertaining enough for the digital world* they must have thought.

I talked the principal into allowing me to introduce a lunchtime chess club and then I began teaching my class on fun Fridays. It was a rocky start, because chess takes a bit of mastering (I tell students they need to play the game at least ten times to grasp the game). The group didn't have that kind of patience, but we made it through several weeks. They began to see that it took analytical thinking and strategy to win the game.

It was not a game of chance.

By the time I left the school in June, the tough boys were coming up saying, "You know, this is a really good game."

"I *know*," I told them. "Just keep it in your life and you will be able to conquer anything."

I can always get children's attention in most countries of the world — whether I know the language or not — by introducing them to the game of chess. They start the game, thinking it's checkers or drafts, but they are usually challenged by its complexity and stick with me for one full session. Within the hour, the students will begin playing on their own.

A couple of sessions later, I teach strategies like commanding the center of the board and castling early in the game. I taught chess in villages where no one spoke a word of English. Smiles and friendship still follow a friendly game.

Two years ago, I had the pleasure of meeting and interviewing one of the women's highest ranked world chess champions who is now living here in the United States. Her name is Susan Polgar. Her sister, Judit Polgar, is currently the highest ranked woman's world grandmaster. Susan is currently a professor at Webster University in Saint Louis, Missouri, and trains the highest ranked men's and women's chess teams to compete around the world. Susan, of course, didn't need to convince me of the benefits of chess.

When I'm asked how I managed to survive for twenty years as a school administrator, I always answer, "I play chess."

My big question to Susan was how early is too early to begin teaching children how to play chess. She answered, "Two or three years old."

I was shocked. I usually started school-age children in third grade.

She told me it was a perfect age to introduce the players and ask them just to put the players on the board and name them. After they learn how to move the players ask them which player could make a square or a triangle and play the game with just those players for a while. She said they learn quickly how to look at the entire board.

I shared with her how often teachers told me they wished they had learned how to play the game. "It's scary how *few* people in America play," I said. I encouraged the game through chess clubs in my district. We had sixteen elementary schools, and by running annual tournaments at the end of each school year, I kept the interest in the game alive, at least for the few students who had been exposed to the game. I ran the tournament for 25 years."

"Well," she answered, "In Armenia, every student plays chess at school every day. And last year, (2018) every Russian student was instructed to include it in their daily school schedule. It has an amazing impact on mathematical thinking. Believe me, I have seen the impact of chess all over the world. I *see* that it changes lives. I have the data from studies showing how it changes analytical thinking and another study that proves it can raise one's IQ."

Armenia glorifies chess players in their country. A grandmaster has the same fame as a sports hero. They start young to get that good. It's amazing how much focus a child would need to start learning chess under the age of five.

When I finished my interview, I shuffled through the internet and found a BBC report on studies tracking the mandatory playing of daily chess on children six and over in Britain. I have taught many six- and seven-year-old students the concept of the game, starting with the question, "How does the game start and how does the game end, including the goal of checkmate?"

Attention span is still an issue at these early ages, as well as maturity with the world of winning and losing. No one wants to see a child fall into a puddle of tears when they can't win a game. Often, I teach very young children by not playing an entire game, but playing to a point where one player is getting the advantage and pointing out how the game might end.

Analytical thinking is one of the most powerful skills we can teach anyone. It is the number one **skill** *employers are looking for in interviews. The basis of this is asking: How do I manage to get myself out of a tight spot when* **losing** *isn't an option?*

In chess, as in life, you only learn how to win by losing and learning what *not* to do next time. "Failure leads to success" is one of the eight keys to success, but little children don't want to lose. This instinct is natural and equal to the same driving force as being first in line. Eventually, they must wrestle with the big conclusion: losing *is* part of the game of chess.

When children learn to lose, they can build the skills to outwit their opponent. There is no cheating in chess (the game itself reinforces the integrity of the game). And we bring the students to the point where they understand there is no crying if one loses the game. The lessons are simple and profound. Go the course — learn those analytical skills that make you pause and look at the whole playing field.

One of the primary skills chess players need is to concentrate on the entire board and see patterns, strategies, and tactics that are unique to each game, a skill that, once learned, can be applied in other important areas. Set up strategies and know who your backup is; this is another skill that will make any student successful in school and in life. No wonder all the ancient royals knew how to play the game early! Age-old knights understood strategies of warfare through playing the game of chess long before they brought an army to battle. Chess is a game in which you can never be too good. You can always learn more. As a teacher, you don't have to fight the battle of children objecting to playing a game at the end of a school day when you incorporate chess.

This past summer, I was invited to play a seven-year-old girl from Moscow, Russia. I made the mistake of telling her she would probably win because I was only an intermediate player and have trained many students who can beat me.

"How often do students play chess in schools in Russia?" I asked her.

"In primary grades, it is two times a week. As we get older, we play every day," she responded.

In my first two games playing my little Russian friend, I could see she had a good beginning game and an aggressive middle game, but I was only able to beat her because I had the better end game. *Young players often believe that capturing many players is the goal of the game.*

I did beat her three times on the first day and I *was* met by a flood of tears. Her mother wanted her to thank me for coming over to play her.

"Why should I thank her? She beat me three times."

"Well, you are an amazing player. You almost had me in that second game. The only way I was able to win was to find a way to get down to your king and checkmate him while you were focused on getting my queen. You will beat me eventually, and when you do, I will be giving you ice cream."

Her parents shared that she learned a lot more than the game of chess over *that* summer.

"She learned that losing is part of playing chess, too." It doesn't have to be devastating. It is simply a game. Just shake hands. The winner says, 'Good game,' and you get into another game. The more you play, the better you get."

As an adult, never give away the game and allow a child to win. It may upset you to see them cry, but if you give away the game, you lose your ability to teach them. Those moments are the ones that can really help a child win in the future. Your integrity is lost from the beginning and those vital opportunities may never happen.

My little friend and I played a half dozen more games before she returned to Moscow. She taught me how to teach her while we played. As a teacher, I know I have done my job when I get to learn from my students. Children always teach me better ways to teach them. Let children learn, they will get better than you and they will need to move onto more difficult players in the future. Students can learn more about life and themselves with every game.

Many teachers I speak to often share that they wish they knew how to play chess. They subscribe to a well-known myth, that someone probably needs to be a genius to play it.

"Not true," I repeatedly tell them. "Playing chess **makes** you smart." That is the slogan of The American Chess Federation.

You don't need to know anything to learn the game. But when you begin playing, you begin thinking differently. I can't tell you how many times I was faced with major life decisions, especially in political arenas, and pictured my next move on a chessboard. *If I do this move toward this goal*, I thought, *I better have a power player behind me to back me up.*

In an article entitled, "Chess is Booming" featured in the *New York Times* September 2022 edition, it talks about the renewed interest in the game of chess as captured by its participants on chess.com. After the Pandemic, in just one year, participants playing in online chess games rose on the site chess.com from a million players to almost five million. Today, it is over twelve million.

In 2020 renewed interest in chess was increased by the miniseries *The Queen's Gambit*, originally written as a novel by author Walter Tevis in 1983. Scott Frank's script about an orphaned female chess prodigy captured a worldwide audience as the most watched series on Netflix, winning it two Golden Globes. Market sales on chessboards went up 100 percent.

Since, many children have become interested in the game of chess, and many schools are seeking **volunteers** to help start chess clubs. (See *Resources* for the link to a *YouTube* video about the school custodian in Maine who coached students to win the State championship.)

Susan Polgard, an international chess grand master has developed several video series for young beginners and follow-up videos for developed players. They are a perfect fit for a parent to learn along with their children on *YouTube*. (*Top Tips for Teaching Kids Chess, Chess for Beginners, The Susan Polgard Method for Scholastic Chess.*)

Summary

Engagement Tips for Parenting
the Next Generation

In Chess, help your pieces so they will help you."

~ Paul Morphy

It is predicted that your child will have at least a dozen or more different skilled jobs in the future. You can't have too many skills to be prepared for the future of work.

Parents will need to provide experiences for skillful growth for their children, focusing on essential life skills. Currently, most schools are not designed to prepare students for the many practical skills they need to survive a future of restructuring industries.

1. Create multiple experiences around skills throughout childhood and teen years. This is a foundation for many future job possibilities. (**Experiences** are the best teacher; they build transferable skills.)

2. Develop the meaning around the importance of the why we learn and go to school. This will help support them in the work world.

3. Encourage children ages ten to eighteen to develop a portfolio they can use toward a future resume that will demonstrate the following: skill development, shadowing, mentorships, apprenticeship experience, internships, businesses, volunteer work, and side hustles.

4. Caution children about the internet: intake and their input. You can think, imagine, or design anything in your mind you want, but if you put it into pictures or words, you own it... as well as the consequences. (*Some consequences can never be erased.*)

5. In early years, have children interview everyone who has a skill or business on how they came to get involved in this business such as: What do you enjoy about your job? What kind of training did you need to have? How much does someone in your job make annually?

6. As a parent, enjoy your child's journey through discovery and experiences, and remember open conversation without judgment is important.

7. A house with no expectations is sad indeed. We want our children to develop a balanced, happy life that leads them to their independence and opportunities for a sustainable future. This includes setting boundaries and having active guided conversations with young adults. (They will always remember your wisdom.)

8. Speak often with children about dreams and jobs. Let them know they don't start at the top. Getting to the top takes hard work. Diplomas are not the end goal! They are a key to open the door to the journey. **Never** share your colorful growing up experiences like "ditching school" with your children; it becomes an

automatic pass for them to do it too. (e.g. Dad did it, so I can.) *Save the sharing until they are over thirty.*

9. Children usually show you what they are ready to learn. As parents, we can pick up on the cues and give them choices. When children are invested in the decision, they will be more open and engaged.

10. Support the 'soft skill" expectations for their first job by modeling these through their formative years: always using good manners, treating everyone with respect, and being a good team player.

Conclusion

Education is the biggest and most important topic in the news today. Current news reports quote that close to 62% of adults in the workforce do not have a bachelor's degree. As a result, government jobs that insisted you needed a college degree before applying are now accepting applicants with good references and those essential work skills. Even airlines have dropped their college degree requirements for pilots. In 2023, over 30,000 "IT" tech graduates found themselves released from what seemed like secure jobs and futures from top industries such as Google, Amazon, Apple, and Microsoft. The headlines stated the companies were restructuring. Restructuring often means letting go of unnecessary paychecks for work that can now be done through other means, like AI (Artificial Intelligence) apps or other new replacement robotic mechanisms.

The pendulum has shifted, and the signs are all around us — flexible skills will hold more weight than diplomas.

This is just the tip of the iceberg for future industry jobs. Technology is predicted to change every five years. Layoffs and restructuring will touch most industries. Flexibility and the confidence that you have many skills and experiences in your pocket shared by caring parents and grandparents is key.

Many changes are coming in industries we see, and many more in industries we are yet to see. It takes broader brush strokes to be prepared for the future, but there is much we can do at home beginning with building character, kindness, values, skill, experiences, but most of all a **work ethic** that will shine a light on all our children are meant to be. Side hustles like coaching tennis or swimming can help foster this. Those music lessons you supplied can help with a live band your adult child plays in on weekends as a paid gig, or those killer cupcakes learned from grandma can fly out the door on their new branding site for local parties.

The message for all parents of school-aged children is this: you are your child's best teacher, and you will never be "too good" at it. It is a 24-hour-a-day job that takes love and consistency and a lifetime of dedication. Keep to your true north, because everything you live and breathe is being taught to your children, from watching you take your run in the morning, to the breakfast you eat, to your love or hate of your work, to family time.

Look around. In the year 2023, the future is ours to see. People in skilled jobs are lacking; many schools at present do not provide what is needed in the United States to quickly enter the work force and many transferable skills will be required of your children as they grow into adults.

Educational institutions are notoriously slow to respond to societal changes, so how do we as parents make sure our children can be successful and responsive as they grow into future jobs? One can go back to Ben Franklin's insight over two hundred years ago when he said, "Experience is the best teacher."

A teacher I spoke with recently stated, "I am teaching fifth grade and a mother wondered when the schools would *ever* start teaching proper letter writing." I responded, "I taught my own children to write formal thank you notes for gifts they received from friends and family. I suggest that as something you might want to start at home."

It's true — still today parents drop their children off at school believing that, magically, the school is teaching them *every* life skill.

As a parent...

It is a critical time to be involved with your child's educational experiences... an experience can be a moment.

Knowing your child's interest and passion will be a key to unlocking future success. It is true your parents and those before them may not have needed direct involvement with their children to help them prepare for future jobs, but today they do, and the earlier the better. The world was much simpler in the past. The job world today is ever-changing.

Now is the perfect time to:

JUMP UP, JUMP IN, but *not* JUMP ON our kids.

Don't be afraid to step in. It is time to expand our roles in our children's lives. They need: a teacher of skills, a mentor to build their life-long learning skills around their interests, and a supporter encouraging their passion.

Everyone wins when they are vested in a child's future. At no other time in history have students been challenged by such huge educational gaps and lack of directional support to jobs, many of which are yet to be imagined.

Resources

Accelerated Reading, Reading Plus. (n.d.). https://www.renaissancelearning.com

California community colleges by tuition cost (2023). (n.d.). Community College
Review - Profiles of USA Community Colleges. Retrieved April 24, 2023, from
https://www.communitycollegereview.com/tuition-stats/california#

(n.d.). Career Zone. Retrieved April 24, 2022, from https://www.careerzone.org

Chess for Beginners with GM Susan Polgar. (n.d.). YouTube.ichess.net

Coalition for Community Schools. https://www.communityschools.org

Custodian teaches students how to sweep their chess competition,
http://www.Youtube.com

Desktop Career Surfer. (n.d.). California Career Resource Network.
https://www.californiacareers.info

Famous Chess Quotes. (n.d.). Chess.com. https://Chess.com

Grit, The Power of Passion and Perseverance, (Pub. Scribner, August 21, 2018).
Angela Duckworth

Guided Pathways in Community Colleges. (n.d.). California Community Colleges.
https://www.cccco.edu

High Frequency Word lists. (n.d.) https://www.readinga-z.com

High School Pathway Programs. (n.d.). greatschool.org. Retrieved March 24, 2023,
from https://www.greatschool.org

Holland code (RIASEC) test. (n.d.). Take a personality test - Open Source Psycho-
metrics Project. https://openpsychometrics.org/tests/RIASEC/

Hollands Code for personalities RIASEC. (n.d.). Career Advice | Career Key.
https://www.careerkey.org

How to play '99' — Gather together games. (n.d.). Gather Together Games.
https://gathertogethergames.com/99game

(n.d.). Job Central. https://www.mystuffjobcentral.org

Kasparov, G. (2010). *How life imitates chess: Making the right moves, from the board to the boardroom.* Bloomsbury Publishing USA.

Kentucky community colleges by tuition cost (2023). (n.d.). Community College Review - Profiles of USA Community Colleges. Retrieved April 24, 2023, from https://www.communitycollegereview.com/tuition-stats/kentucky#

Let's teach kids skills for life | Virgin. (n.d.). Virgin.com. https://www.virgin.com /branson-family/richard-branson-blog/lets-teach-kids-skills-for-life

(2021, April 9). Marilyn Burns Math. https://marilynburnsmath.com/

(n.d.). no title. Retrieved January 17, 2022, from https://www.california careercenter.org

Linked Learning Alliance. linkedlearning.org

Part of the Pathful. Ask questions virtually to industry professionals. (n.d.). Your College & Career Readiness Journey | Pathful. https://www.pathful.com /connect

(n.d.). Pavlovian Classical Conditioning. https://study.com/learn/lesson /pavlov-theory.html

RWS (Real World Scholars) creating EdCorp in schools. (n.d.). Learning in the Real World. https://www.realworld.org

San Diego industry jobs. (2022, September 22). SOCAL Workforce. https://Socalworkforce.org

(n.d.). Wisconsin Department of Public Instruction | . https://dpi.wi.gov/sites /default/files/imce/school-nutrition/pdf/second-chance-breakfast-service -model.pdf

Workforce Partnership: (2021, February). https://www.workforce.org.career -centers

(ST Math) Spatial Temporal Math. (n.d.). https://blogmindresearching.org

Surgeon General's New Advisory About Effects of Social Media Use With Children, https://www.hhs.gov.files

5K Fun/run "Move Your Feet, Before You Eat". (2022, July 14). O'side Turkey Trot - San Diego's Favorite Turkey Trot. https://osideturkeytrot.com

"World of Work". (n.d.). Cajon Valley Union School District / Homepage. https://www.cajonvalley.net

Acknowledgments

I will always be eternally grateful for my sister, who's the voice in my head, my sons and their wives who became my heart and soul, my grandchildren who fill my heart with joy, and *all* my special friends (you know who you are) who have always supported me in my gypsy-style life. Your love and support have allowed me to experience the world and its children.

In addition, very special thanks to everyone who helped me in the development of this message for parents especially: Susie Schaefer, Tiffany Vakilian, Nadia Geagea Pupa, Michelle White, Lisa Shrewsberry, Maddy McMillion, Beth Conard, Corie Slali, Dylan Sershon, Jo Anne Scuderi, Denise Conti, Steve Bessant, Lisa Gill, Erica Cox, Kathy Rohan, April Marie Sheffield, Margaret Malek, Deborah Sandoval, Edward Ochenge Kabaka, all my staff, teachers, and students of Oceanside Unified schools, the San Diego Workforce Partnership, and San Diego County Office of Career Tech Education.

As I mentioned in the forward of this book, I began to write about ways to help parents during the Pandemic but instead diverted to wanting to help parents prepare their children for a completely different future than the world they grew up in.

When I reflect on my passion for teaching, it has always been about what insight, experiences, and skills I could give children in our brief time together that could benefit them in future jobs. I always appreciate those who could connect the *why* we go to school to the big picture: John K Cahalin, Elyse Burden with RWS (Real World Scholars) who created EdCorp entrepreneurships in classrooms around the USA, Devon Vodicka, Chief Executive Officer of Child Center Collaborative, Ed Hildalgo, Innovation and Engagement Advisor and proponent for "The World of Work."

And of course, a special shout out to all my Beta readers: Margaret Malek, Erica Cox, Lisa Gill, Deborah Sandoval, and April Marie Sheffield.

My life in education has been truly my passion and purpose. There wasn't a day I didn't love my job. I am so grateful for all the hundreds of teachers I have had the privilege to work with over my extensive career. *I could always see in each of their faces that it was a calling to be a teacher.* The school was my second home, my wheelhouse. It has been the connective tissue of most of my relationships. Whether fiction or non-fiction, there are stories in all of us that need to be shared as well as messages that need to be passed on.

As for all the children, literally thousands that I have come to know: Bless you and thank you for the memories we shared. Each of you has been a *gift* to my life. You gave me far more than I gave you. You taught me everything I needed to learn.

About the Author

Phyllis T. Morgan is a New Jersey native and published author. She is currently living her dream on a motor yacht in the San Diego Bay as she continues to balance her life with racing sail boats. Her career in education has spread over a fifty-year period, covering three states and several countries, including her eight years as a fifth and sixth grade teacher in Sydney, Australia.

Her last twenty-five years as a leader in Oceanside, California schools steered her to be recognized for many major awards for community and global development, including: Chamber of Congress Administrator of the Year, San Diego Administrator Award for Zero Waste programs, STEM school development, innovative farm to table programs with "Go Green Agriculture," San Diego Administrative Technology Award, San Diego Science Alliance Innovative Principal of the Year, "Prize Principal" by Point Loma Nazarene University, two California Distinguished

School Awards, which earned her the ultimate title of Principal of the Year for Southern California, San Diego and Imperial Valley.

She returned to the district after retiring to work as a college and career consultant with Oceanside and the County of San Diego. She helped develop Career Technical Education (CTE) Pathways that would connect with local industries. Phyllis has long been recognized by fellow educators as a visionary. Long before trends and technology entered the educational space, she incorporated support programs that are vastly used today in education. Her passion to prepare children with experiences for the future is evident throughout this book.

She is the proud mother of two beautiful sons and now six beautiful grandchildren. Phyllis continues to pursue an adventurous life, traveling the world and volunteering for International Volunteer programs in such places as: Croatia, Greece, Portugal, Spain, and West Kenya. In each country, she sets up chess clubs and teaches students about the nuances of life and learning English through this ancient analytical game.

She finished her first novel *Down Under* after being published in the anthology, *The Pivot Project*, and another, *The Path to Purpose* during the Pandemic. She is a member of the San Diego Writers and Editors Guild, The Writer Digest Guild, The Wild Atlantic Writers Association, The Author's Guild, and The Romance Writers Guild of America.

She currently helps support "Kids for Peace," volunteers for adaptive sailing races that support challenged sailors (KMAC and other CYC sponsored sailing races) and continues to give career talks at schools and communities about building skill experiences early in life to be more adaptable for future work. To invite Phyllis to speak at your next event, please email Phyllis T Morgan at: Phyllis.moonscapepress@gmail.com.

See more at: skillfulfutures.com, or contact Phyllis T. Morgan at phyllis.moonscapepress@gmail.com. You can also find Phyllis on LinkedIn, Instagram, Twitter, Facebook, YouTube, and Tik Tok.